C000005835

THE ART OF SUCCESS: LEONARDO DA VINCI

HOW EXTRAORDINARY ARTISTS CAN HELP YOU SUCCEED IN BUSINESS AND LIFE

CASSANDRA GAISFORD

THE ART OF SUCCESS

How Extraordinary Artists Can Help You Succeed in Business
and Life

Book One: Leonardo da Vinci

Cassandra Gaisford, BCA, Dip Psych

PRAISE FOR THE ART OF SUCCESS

"This beautiful book wraps art around business and life and makes each hum with energy and creativity and brings the reader new vitality. This little book is a gem to have in the office and the home bookcase, and for me, because it is so beautiful, I will have it in my handbag - always at hand and safe in the knowledge that wisdom, plain good business sense and creativity are close at hand. "

~ Catherine Sloan, counselor

"This book is a work of art. Art with words. The headings alone got me all jazzed up. The author is a word artist in the best possible way. This is a delightful guide with simple, life-affirming messages that will help anyone succeed in business and in life. I was down in the dumps about something in my life and reading just a few pages of this book lifted me completely out of it. LOVE it!"

~ Amazon Review

"After reading *The Art of Success* and having in mind other books I've read on similar topics, one thing that clearly stands out is that the book is leaned on the life principles of one of the greatest persons of mankind, Leonardo da Vinci. It raises and reflects upon the questions and decisions many of us face in our daily life. Cassandra explain further how to apply these principles of the genius in our lives. I feel really supported and encouraged. It's just magic."

~ Hrvoje Klobucar

"This book is indeed like a shot of espresso... a brilliant inspiring resource that you can pick up when you need some encouragement to keep you moving forward on your journey to success!"

~ Judy McCluskey

"This book will challenge the way you think about success and broaden your mind to a holistic perspective on achievement. I liked how it was easy to digest in bite sized chapters, and all the quotes along the way. I really enjoyed how Cassandra included relationships and balance in the book because I think many high achievers need this perspective."

~ Olivia Gamber

"This is a work to quicken your spirit, pull back the covers of your soul (even if just a little) and open the door to a more authentic and vital you."

~ Amazon Review

"Another wonderful 'how to change your world' from Cassandra full of wise advice helping us make the most of our lives."

~ Coralie Unwin

"I learned much. The book has a compelling energy about it that draws one in and did so again and again as I found myself going back to it to re-read a section and feel inspired."

~ Anon

"This was a great piece of work and I finished the book in one night. It was an easy read and I really enjoyed learning more about Leonardo. I loved how Cassandra created a holistic picture of success and did not ignore any component that is so key to a fulfilling life."

~ Olivia Gamber

"I felt quite inspired, not just once but again and again, as I was in a sense almost caught up and swept along in the flow through the book. You've achieved something very helpful for many of us seeking guidance on how to change ourselves into someone better, more capable, more self-aware, more loveable. And not through lots of techniques (the tips are very helpful though) but somehow through getting back to the basics of knowing ourselves, who we are and where do we fit in the universe. The scope was great too with sufficient detail to stim-ulate further searching for ourselves. The most powerful aspect for me was that to succeed—go within! Discover the true

SELF, the soul and so feel that connection with something much bigger than me, even to cosmic dimensions."

~ Rex

"I read a lot of books on self-help. After a while you can read so many they all start to sound the same. What I love about this book is that it makes you want to slow down and take in each chapter piece by piece. There are so many tidbits of amazing strategies and philosophy that you are drawn in by the passion of the life of Da Vinci. I love the lay out of this book where it discussed seven ways to empower yourself in success, mind, body, spirit, work, relationships, and vision. Each chapter focuses on teaching a new principle to make your life better in so many ways. I also like the challenges at the end of each chapter so you don't just get to read the book but follow through on implementing it into your life and passion as well. A definite read for improving your success, health and overall MINDSET!"

~ Scott Allan

DEDICATION

This book is dedicated to love.

This book is also dedicated to Lorenzo, my Knight Templar,
who encourages and supports me
to make my dreams possible...

And for all my clients
who've shared their dreams with me,
and allowed me to help them achieve amazing feats.

Thank you for inspiring me.

"They will say that I, having no literary skill, cannot properly express that which I desire to treat of, but they do not know that my subjects are to be dealt with by experience rather than by words. And experience has been the mistress of those who wrote well. And so, as mistress, I will cite her in all cases. Though I may not, like them, be able to quote other authors, I shall rely on that which is much greater and more worthy: on experience, the mistress of their Masters."

~ Leonardo da Vinci, *1472*

FOREWORD

As the opening of this book promises, if you're short on time but high on motivation, then this is the book that can help you move toward your success.

It's amazing how much can be packed into a book that can be read in one sitting. But if you do, be prepared to come back to the *Art of Success* again and again because there is not only wisdom on every page, but actionable, immediate steps you can take to make a difference in reaching your own goals and dreams.

This book is like meeting with your best friend—the one who can give you a pep talk or a sharp rap on the head, depending on what you need.

Broken into small, bite-sized segments—you'll soon find yourself jotting notes down, finding someone else so you can share the insights and experience, and even more resources made available to keep you motivated and focused.

Power-packed is the word that came to mind as I was reading, nodding and inspired. Cassandra Gaisford created a real gem in what I have no doubt will be a life-changing series for many people. Don't just take my word for it. Keep reading!

—Mary Buckham, USA Today Best Selling Author and International Writing Craft Instructor

AUTHOR'S NOTE

Realize that everything connects to everything else .

~ Leonardo da Vinci

L eonardo was just like you and I. He suffered at times from self-doubt, he had family hassles, some of his efforts resulted in failure, people jealous of his talent tried to undermine him, money worries meant that at times he had to suck it up and do work he didn't enjoy, and he had to work for bullies and tyrants.

But he didn't let obstacles stop him from doing the work he loved. The pursuit of knowledge born of his own enquiry and experience ultimately led to his success. He also learned from experts he admired, both past and present.

I created the *Art of Success* series to reveal how the success secrets and strategies of extraordinary artists like Leonardo da

Vinci can help people like you and I succeed—personally and professionally. Successful artists have always struggled, but they persevered anyway. And it is this willingness to pursue their calling in the face of many challenges that holds lessons for us all.

Who Is This Book For?

If you want to challenge conventional definitions of success and live a life on your own terms, this book is for you.

If you're an aspiring creative, or an accomplished one, *The Art Of Success* will provide support and encouragement to continue the journey.

If you suffer from fear, doubt, procrastination, or overly seek validation from others, *The Art Of Success* will come to your rescue.

If you're a Type A personality looking for the fastest route to success, *The Art Of Success* will challenge you to experiment with going quickly slowly, to avoid burning out. Or overrunning the turn-off that would lead you down the path less travelled—the route that may lead you to your most enduring success.

Or you might, like me, be passionate about Leonardo da Vinci and all that he achieved, and want to discover his success secrets.

Your Concise Guide to Success

The Art of Success is a concise guide to succeeding in business and in life. My vision was simple: a few short, easy to digest tips for time-challenged people who were looking for inspiration and practical strategies to encourage positive change.

I knew that people didn't need a wad of words to feel inspired, gain clarity and be stimulated to take action.

In coaching and counselling sessions I'd encourage my clients to ask a question they would like answered. The questions could be specific, such as, 'How can I make a living from my passion?' Or vague, for example, 'What do I most need to know?' They were always amazed at how readily answers flowed.

In this era of information obesity the need for simple, life-affirming messages is even more important. If you are looking for inspiration and practical tips, in short, sweet sound bites, this guide is for you.

Similarly, if you are a grazer, or someone more methodical, this guide will also work for you. Pick a section or page at random, or work through the principles sequentially. I encourage you to experiment, be open-minded and try new things. I promise you will achieve outstanding results.

Let experience be your guide, as it was Leonardo's. Give your brain a well-needed break. Let go of 'why' and embrace how you feel or how you want to feel. Honour the messages from your intuition and follow your path with heart.

Laura, who at one stage seemed rudderless career-wise, did just that. She was guided to Principle Seven: Fruitful Collaborations. Following that, her motivation to live and work like those she looked up to sparked a determination to start her own business. It was that simple.

At the time of writing I've just turned to Principle Eight:

Pursue Your Own Truth. It's a timely reminder that no matter what others may think of this book, it works for me. The following quote may also speak to you: "I can't give you the recipe for success but I can failure. Try to please everyone."

How This Book Will Help You

Whenever I'm in a slump or needing an inspirational boost I turn to people who are smarter or more skilled than me for good advice.

I've done the same with qualities I've wanted to develop, like patience. "What would Mother Theresa do now?" I asked many years ago. Mother Theresa wouldn't shout! She wouldn't lose her cool. She'd send loving kindness and smile. And that's what I did whenever I got frustrated.

Leonardo da Vinci was super smart! As I wrote *The Art of Success*, I applied the strategies I'm sharing with you to help me finish this book and make progress with my historical novel, *Mona Lisa's Secret*.

If you've been procrastinating, experiencing self-doubt, feeling fearful, or just getting in your own way, you're in good company, Leonardo's been there. I've been there too—as have many successful people. Guess what, getting in your own way is normal!

I promise there are solutions to the problems you're currently facing—and you'll find them in the pages that follow.

Dig into this book and let Leonardo da Vinci be your mentor, inspiration and guide as he calls forth your passions, purpose and potential.

Through the teachings of Leonardo, extensive research into the mysteries of motivation, success and fulfilment, and my own personal experience and professional success with clients as a holistic therapist, *The Art of Success* will help you accelerate success. Together, Leonardo and I will guide you to where you need to go next, and give you practical steps to achieve success.

I was once told that I had the soul of an artist. Actively discouraged in childhood, for a long time I'd closed off that side of me. I began my career as a bank-teller, then as an accountant, then as a recruitment consultant, followed by more 'business-minded' careers. I even spent time in prison—on a work assignment.

Each time I went further and further away from who I truly was and the things that gave me joy. Leonardo was luckier—he was encouraged to pursue his natural inclination. My hope is that after reading *The Art of Success* you will too.

Whether your calling is the world of commerce, or seeking answers in the stars, it's never too late to be yourself.

Step into this ride joyfully and start creating your best life today.

Step into this ride joyfully and start creating your best life today.

HOW TO USE THIS BOOK

Leonardo was a systems thinker who recognised and valued the interconnectedness of everything. He can teach us many lessons, including the link between passion and inspiration, mental strength, emotional resilience, spiritual power, health and well-being, empowering relationships, smart goals and authentic success.

The *Art of Success* takes a holistic look at what it means, and what it takes, to be successful.

The Eight Principles of Success

I've sectioned The Art of Success into a cluster of principles. Principles aren't constricting rules unable to be shaped, but general and fundamental truths which may be used to help guide your choices.

Let's look briefly at The Eight Principles of Success and what each will cover:

Principle One, "The Call For Success" will help you explore the truth about success and define success on your own terms. You'll discover the rewards and 'realities' of success, and intensify success-building beliefs.

Principle Two, "Empower Your Success," will help you learn why igniting the fire within, love, and heeding the call for passion is the cornerstone of future success. You'll clarify who you really are and who you want to be, discover your elemental, signature strengths, and clarify your passion criteria.

Sight was the sense Leonardo valued above all else. **Principle Three, "Empower Your Vision,"** will help you clarify and visualise what you really want to achieve. You'll then be better able to decide where best to invest your time and energy. You'll also begin exploring ways to develop your life and career in light of your passions and life purpose, maintain focus and bring your vision into successful reality.

Principle Four, "Empower Your Spirit," urges you to pay attention to the things that feed your soul, awaken your curiosity, stir your imagination and create passion in your life.

Principle Five, "Empower Your Mind," looks at ways to cultivate a success mindset. You'll also identify strategies to overcome obstacles and to maximise your success, and ways to work less but achieve more to gain greater balance and fulfilment.

Your health is your wealth yet it's often a neglected part of success. **Principle Six, "Empower Your Body,"** recognises the importance of a strong, flexible and healthy body to your mental, emotional, physical and spiritual success.

You'll be reminded of simple strategies which reinforce the importance of quality of breath, movement, nutrition and sleep. Avoiding burnout is also a huge factor in attaining and sustaining success. When you do less, and look after yourself more, you can and will achieve success.

Principle Seven, "Empower Your Relationships" will help you boost your awareness of how surrounding yourself with your vibe tribe will fast-track your success, and when it's best to go it alone.

The Art of Success ends with **Principle Eight, "Empower Your Work"** emphasises the role of authenticity and being who you are. You'll also learn how to 'fake it until you make it' and be inspired by others success. Importantly you'll learn how following your own truth will set you free.

How To Best Enjoy This Book

Think of *The Art of Success* like a shot of espresso. Sometimes one quick hit is all it takes to get started. Sometimes you need a few shots to sustain your energy. Or maybe you need a bigger motivational hit and then you're on your way.

You're in control of what works best for you. Go at your own pace, but resist over-caffeinating. A little bit of guidance here-and-there can do as much to fast-track your success, as consuming all the principles in one hit.

Skim to sections that are most relevant to you, and return to familiar ground to reinforce home-truths. But most of all enjoy your experience.

Your Challenge

"I love your works to date—provocative and supportive at the

same time," a gentleman who'd read my *Mid-Life Career Rescue* books wrote to me.

To provoke is to incite or stimulate. It's the reason I've included open-ended questions and calls to action in each guide. The best questions are open, generative ones that don't allow for 'yes/no' answers; rather they encourage you to tap into your higher wisdom, intuition, or go in search of answers—as Leonardo did.

Dive Deeper With The Art of Success Workbook

The Art of Success print book is also available as a workbook, with space to write your responses to the challenges within the book.

Expand Your Learning—Follow My Blog

Gain more insights—signup to my newsletter and follow my blog—navigate to here www.cassandragaisford.com

Inspirational Quotes To Support and Empower

Sometimes all it takes is one encouraging word, one timely bit of advice to awaken your power within. Throughout *The Art of Success* I've balanced Leonardo's wisdom with feminine strength —choosing from a wide range of super-capable women, historical and current, young and old.

Women who shared Leonardo's interests and also had to overcome significant obstacles on the way to success. Find out more about their stories, navigate to the post, *The obstacle race: how to be successful despite setbacks,* on my blog.

Be Empowered

Empowerment is defined as giving power or authority to someone or something—who better to decide who assumes this power and sovereign authority than you.

Empowered people do what they need to do to assume mastery over their thoughts, feelings, emotions and things that affect their lives.

Empowered people are successful people because they live life on their terms. They do the things that really matter to them and those they love.

Empowered people are resilient in the face of setbacks, disappointments or attacks and they're flexible enough to tackle obstacles in the path.

Like Leonardo da Vinci, they recognise they are the experts and sovereign authority in their lives. They learn from, and surround themselves with other empowered successful people. They back themselves, even when they don't succeed.

Are you ready to heed the call for success and define success on your own terms?

LET'S GET STARTED!

PRINCIPLE ONE: THE CALL FOR SUCCESS

WHAT IS SUCCESS?

I wish to work miracles.

~Leonardo da Vinci

Modern definitions of success are often too narrowly defined. Success is more than climbing up the corporate ladder. It's more than a big shiny car, or owning the latest and greatest. It's more than the number of likes you have on Facebook.

Success includes maintaining good health, energy and enthusiasm for life, fulfilling relationships, creative freedom, well-being, peace of mind, happiness and joy. Success also includes the ability to achieve your desires—whatever these may be.

Success is living life on your terms.

Leonardo was driven to self-actualise—to fulfil his talents and potential, and achieve his life purpose.

Success meant following his curiosity and the freedom to

think, be and do as he chose. His success came from creatively expressing his most important beliefs and values, and sharing his knowledge with the world.

YOUR CHALLENGE

What does success mean to you?

How will you know when you have succeeded?

Imagine how our culture, how our lives, will change when we begin valuing go-givers as much as we value go-getters.

~ Arianna Huffington, businesswoman

WHAT CAN SUCCESS DO?

The caterpillar which through the care exercised in weaving round itself its new habitation with admirable design and ingenious workmanship, afterwards emerges from it with beautiful painted wings, rising on these towards heaven.

~ Leonardo da Vinci

Many people struggle to achieve because they're not motivated by success. But being successful isn't just about obtaining worldly possessions, status or glory.

Success is achieved by putting energy and effort toward something you desire. Knowing why you want something is just as important as knowing what you want.

ACHIEVING SUCCESS ON YOUR TERMS:

- Helps you lead a richer life
- Is an indispensable part of fulfilment
- Helps you grow
- Energises you
- Liberates you
- Opens up fresh horizons
- Boosts your health and helps you live longer
- Will change your life and the lives of those who matter most to you

Your Challenge

Why is succeeding important to you?

My mother would always remind me: 'Where you are is not who you are.' I grew up in a poor neighbourhood in New York City. My mother saw education as the way up and out for her children. It didn't take long for me to see the wisdom in her beliefs.

~ Ursula Burns, engineer and CEO

SUCCESS FOR ALL

Remember to acquire diligence rather than rapidity.

~ Leonardo da Vinci

Everybody is capable of success, but many people think they're not. Some people believe they're too young to be taken seriously; others that when they hit midlife they've left it too late to succeed.

Successful people come in all shapes, races, ages and stages. And sometimes the greatest successes follow the greatest failures.

To succeed you have to believe it's possible for you—even if it means faking it until you make it and realise it's true. A slow and bumpy road is the route to success for many.

Leonardo's seemingly meteoric rise to success was based on slow, incremental steps, dodging obstacles, fuelled by self-belief and constant and earnest effort.

Your Challenge

What great works might reside inside of you?

What steps, no matter how small, could you begin to take?

Your success will not be determined by your gender or your ethnicity, but only on the scope of your dreams and your hard work to achieve them.

~ Dame Zaha Mohammad Hadid, architect

YOU'RE NEVER TOO OLD OR YOUNG TO MAKE IT BIG

What is fair in men, passes away, but not so in art.

~ Leonardo da Vinci

You're never too old to become legendary. At the time of writing this book Leonardo is forever young at 564—immortalised in our minds and hearts and still impacting science, technology and creativity.

He never let age define his potential for success. He was fifteen when he was apprenticed to Andrea del Verrocchio in 1467—considered old at the time to start his career.

Leonardo was 37 when he began studying anatomy in 1489; 43 when he began The Last Supper in 1495; 44 when he illustrated mathematician Fra Luca Pacioli's *De divina proportione* (On the Divine Proportion).

He was 46 when he attempted a flying machine; 50 when he

became Cesare Borgia's military engineer; and 51 when he began the Mona Lisa in 1503.

At the 'old' age of 55 Leonardo was appointed court painter and engineer by Louis XII, King of France. When he began his last known work and one of his most enigmatic and famous paintings, St John the Baptist, he was 63. Only a few years later, aged 67 he would die legend says, peacefully in the arms of the King of France. And he's still making it big!

Your Challenge

If you believe your age is a barrier to success look for examples where the opposite is true

I never thought I'd be successful. It seems in my own mind that in everything I've undertaken I've never quite made the mark. But I've always been able to put disappointments aside. Success isn't about the end result; it's about what you learn along the way.

~ Vera Wang, fashion designer

REALITY CHECK ON SUCCESS

No sooner is Virtue born than Envy
comes into the world to attack it.

~ Leonardo da Vinci

S uccess is not always fun. Like anything worthwhile, pursuing success often involves great commitment, hard work and sacrifice.

Successful people are prepared to give up things, albeit it temporarily, to live a more passionate and prosperous life. Successful people are prepared to stand out from the crowd, take risks and cope with failure.

The journey to success isn't always glamorous; it's often hard work, with long hours, little thanks and creeping doubt that anyone will appreciate the tireless effort you so passionately put into what you do. You may be, as Leonardo was, attacked by those envious of your achievements.

But the compensation is a bigger, fuller, more interesting life, and the potential to create an enduring legacy.

Your Challenge

What are you prepared to trade-off to be more successful?

What are you prepared to change in your life? What would stop you?

Reserve your right to think, for even to think wrongly is better than not to think at all.

~ Hypatia of Alexandria, astronomer

YOUR BODY BAROMETER

The deeper the feeling, the greater the pain.

~ Leonardo da Vinci

The more you truly care about something, the deeper the consequences can be when you don't act on your desires.

When you aren't true to yourself and you don't do the things you aspire to do your mental, emotional and spiritual health can suffer.

Common signs of neglecting the call for success and forsaking your ambitions can include: tiredness, depression, anxiety, irritability, and strained personal relationships. In short, you're lovesick—starved of the things that spark joy.

The body never lies, but many people soldier on ignoring the obvious warning signs. It's easy to rationalise these feelings away, But the reality is your mind, body and soul is screaming out for more. Have the courage to say 'yes' to pursuing a more liberating alternative.

Your Challenge

When you feel unfulfilled, bored, unchallenged and demotivated what do you notice? How does this differ from times when you feel the fear but love life passionately anyway?

I've been absolutely terrified every moment of my life—and I've never let it keep me from doing a single thing I wanted to do.

~ Georgia O'Keeffe, artist

LIVE A SIGNIFICANT LIFE

No counsel is more trustworthy than that which is given upon ships that are in peril.

~ Leonardo da Vinci

Regret because of a life not lived significantly is a major source of depression, stress and anger for many people.

You only get one shot at life. Don't spend it regretting opportunities you never took and dreams you never lived. Turn moments of peril into catalysts for change in your quest for significance.

Leonardo was often in peril but he mastered the art of creating solutions and turning calamity into good fortune.

That's not to say there weren't days when he truly despaired, when his attempts at innovation failed, when invaders overran the cities where he lived forcing him to flee, when his creations were rejected, destroyed or had to be abandoned.

During all these times, fuelled by his desire to live a significant life, he kept moving forward.

Your Challenge

How could exposure to injury, loss or destruction fuel your motivation to succeed?

If you only had one year to live what would you regret never having been or done? How can you heed the call for significance and pursue your heart's desire?

I believe that every single event in life happens in an opportunity to choose love over fear.

~ Oprah, businesswoman

ESCAPE THE COMFORT RUT

You will never have a greater or lesser dominion than that over yourself...the height of a man's success is gauged by his self-mastery.

~ Leonardo da Vinci

Many people trade off their deeper passions for material comforts and status that can only ever give fleeting satisfaction. Others get stuck in the comfort rut, trapped by the familiarity of what they know. Outwardly, they appear successful but in fact they are deeply unfulfilled.

We all like to be comfortable, but the comfort rut is like wearing old shoes—you just keep putting them on because they feel familiar. But in the deepest part of your heart you know they're full of holes.

Are you too comfortable—stagnating, not growing, nor challenging or exciting yourself? Perhaps it's the fear of the unknown, or starting over, failing or succeeding. Fear is part of the human condition. It reminds you you're alive. But it doesn't have to stop you from succeeding.

Leonardo continually reinvented himself. He strove to master himself—his thoughts, his emotions, his behaviours throughout the change process.

Success equalled growth, aligning with his soul's purpose, taking inspired action he found interesting, meaningful, fulfilling and intriguing.

Being true to your self, and honouring the passion of your soul, can be the most comfortable feeling of all.

Your Challenge

How will fulfilling your potential feel to you? How could gaining more self-mastery benefit your life and boost your success?

I will never give myself the luxury of thinking 'I've made it.' I'm not the same as I was 20 years ago, but I always set the bar higher.

~ Dame Zaha Mohammad Hadid, architect

PRINCIPLE TWO: EMPOWER YOUR SUCCESS

THE POWER OF PASSION

If there's no love, what then?

~ Leonardo da Vinci

Without love you don't have energy. Without energy you have nothing.

When people are pursuing something they are passionate about their drive and determination is infinite. They become like pieces of elastic able to stretch to anything and accommodate any setback. People immobilised by fear and passivity snap like a twig. They lack resilience.

Passion gives people a reason for living and the confidence and drive to pursue their dreams. Leonardo was a man of many loves and deep obsessions. These passions imbued him with infinite energy—powering his creativity, courage, resolve and tenacity.

As Leonardo once said, "No labour is sufficient to tire me."

Even when he was exhausted by life, his passion sustained him.

Your Challenge

What will passion do for you?

The really important stuff is not in my résumé. It's what has gone on almost unnoticed in the secret chambers of the heart.

~ Isabel Allende, author

FIND YOUR ELEMENT

Why go about puffed up and pompous, dressed and decorated with [the fruits], not of their own labours, but of those of others.

~ Leonardo da Vinci

Leonardo's father recognised his exceptional gift for drawing and helped him hone his talent by apprenticing him to Andrea del Verrocchio, a master painter, sculptor, and engineer.

However, Leonardo also self-taught his way to excellence, learning new skills and tackling subjects he passionately wanted to understand but had little knowledge of.

Have you found your point of brilliance? Maybe you're exceptional in drawing, dancing, cooking, or some other field. If that talent is combined with your deepest interests, values, ambitions, and joy that's where you ought to focus.

Whether you know your elemental strengths already or you're at a loss, it's equally important to try new things.

If you don't branch out from what you have already mastered you cannot grow. You may discover a point of brilliance you never knew you possessed. In humans, as there is in hills, sometimes there's a vein of gold that you never knew you owned.

Your Challenge

One way to discover your strongest skills and natural talents is to ask people close to you, "What's my superpower?"

Notice all the things you love to do while expressing your unique talents and list past activities and accomplishments that accurately reflect these abilities

What are some possible ways that expressing your qualities, talents, and skills may fulfil current or future needs? How can you serve?

Pick the places that you want to be great, that you want to focus your energies on and do that—understanding that you're probably not going to be great at everything.

~ Ursula Burns, CEO

YOUR SOUL'S DESIRE

*Men who desire nothing but material riches are absolutely devoid
of that wisdom which is the food and the only true riches of the
mind. So much worthier is the soul than the body, so much nobler
are the possessions of the soul than those of the body.*

~ Leonardo da Vinci

L eonardo described himself as an inventor—it was
fundamental to his success. He was a visionary, always
searching to understand what was and what could be. In his
quest to create and invent he sought knowledge and wisdom
above all else. He sought to fill his soul and he sought to be of
service to the world, advancing science and other realms in the
process.

Acquiring material riches wasn't high on his list of priorities. In
life as in chess forethought wins. Decide what you really want,
what you are prepared to give up for it and what your priorities
will be.

Your Challenge

If you're struggling to clarify what it is you really want notice the times your soul comes alive. Notice what excites and interests you, and keep these clues to passion in an inspirational journal.

Passion, love, bliss or joy—whatever name it goes by—is hard to define but easy to see and feel. Your body will change quickly when the richness of your soul finds you.

Here's just a few of her clues:

- A burning desire, hunger, sense of excitement or feeling of inspiration
- A state of arousal—a racing heart, light-headedness, sweaty palms, butterflies, breathlessness
- A feeling of limitless energy
- A clarity of vision
- A sense of purpose and caring deeply
- A feeling of contentment.

*I don't believe you can ever really cook
unless you love eating.*

~ Nigella Lawson, celebrity chef

ACQUIRE KNOWLEDGE

Learning never exhausts the mind.

~ Leonardo da Vinci

L eonardo was driven to understand how things worked. Through his understanding he was able to excel in his chosen fields, innovate and achieve what many believed impossible.

By studying how birds flew he prophesied one day, 'Man will fly through the air but will not move.' Isn't that what we do when we sit on a plane?

He devoured so many sources of knowledge including: reading ancient texts, studying people and places, writing and drawing to deepen his understanding, hands-on knowledge: making models, prototypes, post-mortem examination, experimentation, travelling and learning about others cultures, mentors—past and present, studying artefacts and symbols, and channelling divine intelligence.

Your Challenge

To achieve success take a leaf out of Leonardo's journal and acquire knowledge; self-knowledge; knowledge of others you admire; knowledge of the people, places, things that fascinate, excite, intrigue, or arouse your curiosity

Gain new knowledge by breaking free of your comfort rut and seek new experiences. Be experimental. It may take a few different experiences to finally find your happy place.

One of the greatest gifts my brother and I received from my mother was her love of literature and language. With their boundless energy, libraries open the door to these worlds and so many others.

~ Caroline Herschel, astronomer

TEACH WHAT YOU WANT TO LEARN

Feathers will raise men,
as they do birds toward heaven.

~ Leonardo da Vinci

Leonardo found purpose and fulfilment in teaching. As have other extremely successful men and women in possession of curious minds, and ennobled with a love of learning. Polymath Tim Ferris, for example, sees himself not as a wealthy entrepreneur but as a teacher.

"It's not how much money we make that ultimately makes us happy between nine and five. It's whether or not our work fulfils us. Being a teacher is meaningful," Malcolm Gladwell writes in *Outliers: The Story of Success.*

Leonardo's feathers of higher learning were the quills with which he wrote his notes. He believed, and knew from experience, the tremendous power of books and words to create miraculous flights of the mind.

He wrote about what he wanted to learn, and found extraordinary success, sharing that knowledge with others.

In coaching and counselling sessions with clients when they say they don't know how to get unstuck, or how to find answers, I gently encourage them to consider writing a blog post I, or they, could share with other people who may also be stuck. It's incredible how the thought of helping others motivates them. And in turn, they help themselves.

Your Challenge

Teach what you want to learn—blog, video, paint, write a song or piece of music, write a book or create some art, create a course, host a seminar or speak at a conference or forum, Youtube or anything else that inspires and challenges you

Enjoy the 'helper's high'—the flow of positive endorphins when you step out of your comfort zone and inspire others

Let us remember: One book, one pen, one child,
and one teacher can change the world.

~ Malala Yousafzai, Noble Peace laureate

LOVE FERVENTLY

*The love of anything is the offspring of knowledge, love being more
fervent in proportion as knowledge
is more certain.*

~ Leonardo da Vinci

Conventional science teaches that the main role of the
heart is to pump blood around your body. But that's just
a tiny part of the heart's power.

Your heart has an intelligence far greater than the brain. Scientific studies also confirm that your heart has the biggest and
most powerful electromagnetic field.

But the heart, like any major organ needs nourishment to
perform miracles. Feed and oxygenate your heart with all the
things you love.

True fervent love is not something you can turn on and off like
a tap. It is an obsession so consuming it feeds your soul. It can

be as tangible as a vocation, or a house or as intangible as a dream or an idea. You could be in love with anything.

Here's a few of the things Leonardo loved with a passion:

- Knowledge
- A cause
- Analysing and understanding things
- Books
- Technology
- The future
- A belief
- An idea
- Freedom

Your Challenge

What captures your heart's interest and attention? List as many things as you can that you love passionately

People feed off passions—not professions. Become a Love Mark and magnetise opportunities toward you. You may want to read more about how to be a love mark in my book *Mid-Life Career Rescue: Employ Yourself.*

I think sometimes that people assume because I'm on television I'm an expert, but I think the whole point of what I do is that I'm not and I don't have any training. My approach isn't about a fancy ingredient or style. I cook what I love to eat.

~ Nigella Lawson, celebrity chef

UNDERSTAND THE RULES

He who loves practice without theory is like the sailor who boards a ship without a rudder and compass and never knows where he may cast.

~ Leonardo da Vinci

If you want to fast-track your success in any endeavour you need to understand the tried-and-proven rules of your chosen field or object of affection.

Leonardo excelled by zealously studying, testing and documenting everything he wanted to master. Always questioning everything, he would take knowledge commonly held to be true and subject it to his own rigorous experimentation.

At times he would disregard the rules entirely, innovating and breaking new ground, and sometimes failing before discovering success.

In this way he pioneered new discoveries, continually improved his work, created a point of difference and mastered his domain through his theory-based beliefs, and willingness to systematically experiment.

"I know that many will call this useless work; and they will be those of whom Demetrius declared that he took no more account of the wind that came out their mouth in words, then of that they expelled from their lower parts," Leonardo once challenged.

Your Challenge

What rules and principles do you need to learn?

What rules and principles do you need to break?

What evidence-based explanations do you have for the beliefs or rules you follow? How might the opposite also be true? How can you adjust your thinking?

Always believe in your work—it will carry you through any difficult situation, but learn to adjust your thinking every once in a while to fit the moment. Never give up. You won't always get everything right every time—but you have to keep trying. Have the commitment to persevere.

~ Dame Zaha Mohammad Hadid, architect

FIND YOUR PURPOSE

Make your work to be in keeping with your purpose.

~ Leonardo da Vinci

Leonardo found deep meaning and purpose in understanding the natural world, sharing the knowledge he found to be true, and being of service to the advancement of humanity.

In learning more about the human body he aided medical advancements. In learning more about the laws of vision and perspective he was able to bring paintings to life.

By mastering the art of mechanics he sought to protect and aid the defence of cities and people important to him.

Everything he committed to was done with purpose.

Given that you spend so much of your life working and you're living longer too, it's even more important to pursue your calling. Need convincing?

Benefits of working and living with purpose include:

- Tapping into your life's purpose gives you an edge, firing the flames of passion, enthusiasm, drive and initiative needed to succeed
- A sense of purpose can give you the courage, tenacity and clarity of vision needed to thrive
- Purpose fuels the embers of flagging motivation and helps fuel latent dreams
- A sense of purpose can lead you to the work you were born to do
- Discovering your true calling opens you up to the dreams the Universe has for you—bigger than you can dream for yourself.

Your Challenge

What life experiences give your life meaning and purpose?

How could your purpose benefit you and others?

It is in giving that I connect with others, with the world and with the divine.

~ Isabel Allende, author

FIND (AND FACE) YOUR WEAKNESS

Look carefully what part is most ill-favoured in your person and take particular pains to correct it in your studies.

~ Leonardo da Vinci

Your biggest weakness can be your greatest strength at times, but equally your greatest strength can be your greatest weakness.

The most important step is self-awareness. Knowing exactly where you need to develop skill or minimise ill-effect will help you develop an effective strategy for success.

Arguably, one of Leonardo's flaws was not finishing the things he started. While there may be many valid reasons for this, some say that Leonardo regretted leaving so many things undone.

Georgio Vasari claims shortly before Leonardo died he said, "I have offended God and mankind by not working on my art as I should have done."

Discovering and taming your own weaknesses can be challenging for several reasons. You may lack objectivity. Other people around you may not be willing to give you honest feedback, or you may stubbornly refuse to deal with your flaws.

Your Challenge

Conduct your own investigation to decide if your weaknesses are holding you back

Notice what you are avoiding. Sometimes the things you're putting off could be a sign of something you haven't mastered

Analyse feedback. Review and look for patterns in any assessments and feedback from others. Is there a common theme?

Ask for honesty. Explain that you're wanting to work on your areas for development

Study past failures. Look back at things that didn't go so well and work out why you didn't succeed

Handle it. You can't improve unless you're open to critical, constructive feedback. If something in you is triggered, or your self-esteem and confidence is dealt a blow, put energy into learning how to deal positively with criticism

Leonardo wasn't perfect. I'm not perfect. You're not perfect. No one is perfect. There is always room for improvement if you want to grow.

Anyone who achieves a certain level of success is first and foremost competing against themselves. And for me the idea that I could always do better, learn more, learn faster, is something that came from skating. But I carried that with me for the rest of my life.

~ Vera Wang, fashion designer

AFFIRM FOR SUCCESS

Experience is the mother of all Knowledge.

~ Leonardo da Vinci

Leonardo was just like you and I. He made mistakes, faced many obstacles, endured hardships—including envy, false accusations, exile, and the rejection and destruction of many of his most beloved works. And he was human—he experienced self-doubt like the rest of us.

There were times when he may have felt like giving up—and sometimes did. But his courage and persistence to remain true to himself in the face of adversity can inspire us all.

One of the secrets to his success, one that strengthened his will was his use of empowering affirmations. In his notebook he urged himself on:

- I do not depart from my furrow
- Every obstacle is destroyed through rigour

- Obstacles do not bend me
- As you cannot do what you want, want what you can do
- I shall continue
- I am never weary of serving.

RESILIENCE in the face of adversity is a critical determinant of success in business and life.

Your Challenge

What affirmations can you create to sustain you in the face of self-doubt or questioning of the value of your efforts? How can you cheerlead your way to success?

Plant your affirmations deeper by framing them emotionally. Instead of, "Obstacles do not bend me", experiment with "I feel strong in the face of obstacles—they do not bend me." This engages your heart-centre so that deeper, more resilient changes can take root

It was such a depressing time. I didn't look very depressed maybe but it was really dire. I made a conscious decision not to stop, but it could have gone the other way.

~ Dame Zaha Mohammad Hadid, architect

BE AMBITIOUS

Escape the cauldron.

~ Leonardo da Vinci

Many people struggle to achieve because they're not ambitious. Being ambitious may stir your fears—fear of success, failure, regret, disappointment, or loss. Or it may trigger a fear of standing out. You may associate ambition with negative traits, like aggression.

Reframe ambition and look to your heroes and heroines. As Leonardo once said, "I want to create miracles." If that's not ambitious I don't know what is. He wasn't hard and aggressive —he was focused on escaping the fires of mediocrity and he kept his vision fixed on success.

Your Challenge

When you think of someone ambitious that you admire who comes to mind?

What qualities do they possess? How could you copy-cat or borrow these qualities and apply them to help you succeed?

Keep your ambition a secret—avoid the critics and those who may knock your confidence. When you start to flap your ambition wings other people may feel threatened or jealous

It's cool to be ambitious. People want to hang out with ambitious, successful people. Pursue your big audacious goals! Do the things you think you can't. Achieve the impossible.

Read more tips to stimulate your ambition on my blog.

The world is in perpetual motion, and we must invent the things of tomorrow. One must go before others, be determined and exacting, and let your intelligence direct your life. Act with audacity.

~ Madame Veuve Cliquot, businesswoman

PLAN FOR SUCCESS

God sells us all things
at the price of labor.

~ Leonardo da Vinci

Planning and effort prevents poor performance. This is such a powerful message when it comes to our goals, especially if you're someone who equates planning with feeling controlled. You may be looking to the future thinking, "Someday! Someday I will achieve that."

How can you be assured that things will happen if you don't plan your action steps effectively, efficiently and productively?

So many people end their lives disappointed that things didn't come to fruition. "Why didn't it happen for me? Why, when it happens for other people." Successful people don't sit at home waiting for things to happen. They go out and conquer things.

If you're sitting back waiting for 'someday' you have a problem —you think you have time!

Your Challenge

Set one goal for yourself and start breaking it down into bite size chunks. If you want to generate $100,000 out of your business in a year what do you need to do to get there?

If you want to start a new relationship, or improve the one you've got, develop your success strategy. Your efforts will be repaid in exchange for your labor and your courage to try.

Do the one thing you think you cannot do. Fail at it. Try again. Do better the second time. The only people who never tumble are those who never mount the high wire. This is your moment. Own it.

~ Oprah, businesswoman

BE SOLUTION-FOCUSED

Look at the light and consider its beauty. Blink your eye and look at it again: what you see was not there at first, and what was there is no more.

~ Leonardo da Vinci

One of the most common questions people who answered The Art of Success questionnaire said they would ask both Leonardo da Vinci and I—is how do we keep going in the face of obstacles? What gives us persistence?

One of the essential things is believing your goal or dream is worth fighting for. Do you want it bad enough? Does it fill your soul with fire? Without passion in your heart you won't have energy, making it hard to get started—let alone to keep going.

But even with fire in your soul, you need to fan the flames of desire with a healthy dose of optimism, and lavish doses of self-soothing, in the face of setbacks.

I'm just like you. I feel defeated sometimes. Worn out. Frustrated. And sometimes I wonder if it's all just too hard. Leonardo did too.

Sometimes we have no idea how to overcome the obstacles we face. But—after allowing ourselves to feel natural emotions such as despondency, frustration, and despair—we must get on with generating solutions.

Leonardo loved solving problems. He thrived on challenge. He didn't like anything getting the better of him. And he loved to succeed—qualities you can cultivate.

Your Challenge

Go on a problem-free diet. Talk and proactively look for solutions

Feeling fearful? Feel the fear and act 'as if' you are confident, courageous and full of massive self-belief

I don't think of myself as a poor deprived ghetto girl who made good. I think of myself as somebody who from an early age knew I was responsible for myself, and I had to make good.

~ Oprah Winfrey, businesswoman

PRINCIPLE THREE: EMPOWER YOUR VISION

BEGIN WITH THE END IN SIGHT

There are three classes of people: those who see. Those who see when they are shown. Those who do not see.

~ Leonardo da Vinci

"He is thinking of the end before he has begun the work," complained Pope Leo X. "This man will do nothing at all!"

Pope Leo X, born Giovanni di Lorenzo de' Medici, had commissioned a painting and was vexed to see that Leonardo began by distilling certain herbs and oils to create a new form of varnish to put over the artwork when completed.

Yet as Stephen Covey made famous in his influential book, *The Seven Habits of Highly Successful People,* beginning with the end in mind (seeing the project completed) and sharpening the saw (preparing your tools of success) are important preparatory steps, steps that people impatient for results often neglect.

Beginning with the end in sight, is also a powerful way of strengthening motivation, persistence and perseverance. The future does belong to those believe in the beauty of their dreams and schemes

Your Challenge

Let desire propel you forward by acting as if, seeing as if, feeling as if, tasting as if, touching as if your success has already been achieved.

- You attract the things you think about—out of sight, out of mind. Here's a few ways to keep your goals in sight:
- Visualise your preferred future. Create a vision, success, or manifestation collage—or do as I once did and create a manifestation fridge
- Borrow from your ultimate future. Remind yourself daily of the benefits success will bring
- A year from now where do you want to be? Looking back, if you had started one year ago where would you be today? It's not too late to start.

DON'T BE DISHEARTENED or discouraged if other people can't see what you can see, or they don't believe in your vision. If you can see it, and you can believe it, in time you can achieve it.

When you take a flower in your hand and really look at it, it's your world for the moment. I want to give that world to someone else. Most people in the city rush around so, they have no time to look at a flower. I want them to see it whether they want to or not.

~ Georgia O'Keeffe, artist

JOURNAL

Dimmi—tell me…tell me whether…
tell me how things are…tell me if there was ever.

~ Leonardo da Vinci

Histon has been made richer by the many successful men and women who kept daily journals. Marcus Aurelius, Benjamin Franklin, and Julia Cameron, playwright and author of phenomenal bestseller *The Artist's Way*, all understand the transformational power of journals. As did Leonardo.

He was a prolific recorder of all things that interested and excited him. He maintained over 13,000 pages of scientific notes and drawings on natural philosophy, life, travel and mysteries.

"Preserve these sketches as your assistants and masters," he once wrote in his journal.

His notebooks not only log his interests and the things he

witnessed with his own eyes, but it was also a medium by which he channelled his intuition. His journals further evidence his belief in the existence of universal knowledge and divine intelligence.

He habitually doodled the word 'dimmi' which translates 'tell me', or 'speak to me', asking for answers and by posing questions. Today we commonly refer to this as seeking intuitive insight.

Journalling helped Leonardo clarify his thinking, affirm his goals, make sense of everything, understand, learn, and grow.

His journals supported him throughout his life—helping him overcome doubts and fears and achieve self-mastery.

Your Challenge

How can your journals be both servant and master in the journey to success?

Do you already have a journal? Do you record the present and dream of the future. Have you made journalling a daily habit?

Write what should not be forgotten.

~ Isabel Allende, author

THE ART OF SUCCESS

Art is the queen of all sciences communicating knowledge to all the generations of the world.

~ Leonardo da Vinci

After enduring years of disappointment, losses and failures, and following the shunning of his work by Pope Leo X in Rome, Leonardo left Italy. Taking one of his most famous paintings with him—the portrait of Mona Lisa—he took up residence with Francis I, the King of France.

The power of exceptional works of heart transcend the rational mind. They transcend time and space. They immortalise knowledge that sustains, empowers, encourages and inspires.

Leonardo refused to be parted from his portrait of Mona Lisa. She was his queen—embodying and communicating the knowledge he valued most.

Many people underestimate the power of art. But it's not lost on the wealthy and successful who surround themselves with quality pieces. But art needn't be expensive to work its magic. You don't need to even own it.

"Art is how spirit speaks to you," a psychic once told me. And it's true. It's the reason I began writing my historical novel *Mona Lisa's Secret*.

It's also the reason I persevered despite feeling overwhelmed by the enormity and responsibility of tackling writing about such an iconic painting.

One day, after a lengthy period of giving in to resistance, while visiting an exhibition of Renaissance paintings a portrait of a young nun spoke to me, "What are you waiting for," she challenged. "You're not like me. You have your liberty. You have choice."

Your Challenge

What visual cue or icon can you carry with you to power your success and embody the truths and values you cherish most?

How does it speak to you?

We do not judge great art.
It judges us.

~ Caroline Herschel, astronomer

BRAINSTORM IDEAS

By indistinct things the mind is stimulated
to new inventions.

~ Leonardo da Vinci

Are you lost for ideas? As Martin Kemp notes in *The Marvellous Works of Nature and Man*, the foundation of many of Leonardo's greatest works began in a 'brainstorm' of dynamic sketching, scribbled in a frenzy of creative impatience.

Letting go of rigidly planning, and in its place allowing ideas to flow with the flexibility of preparatory sketching became the norm for later centuries.

But it was introduced almost single-handedly by Leonardo. Many of his ideas and inventions were triggered by looking for patterns, meaning and significance in seemingly unrelated ideas or objects.

Leonardo once wrote, "Do not despise my opinion, when I

remind you that it should not be hard for you to stop sometimes and look into the stains of walls, or the ashes of a fire, or
clouds, or mud or like places, in which, if you consider them
well, you may find really marvellous ideas...*because by indistinct things the mind is stimulated to new inventions.*"

When I was at architecture school took a class teaching furni-
ture design. My tutor, frustrated by my linear and rational
thinking, encouraged me to pair insects with tables to generate
more interesting designs. My mind expanded—suddenly a
table no longer needed to be square and have four legs!

Your Challenge

Whenever you feel blocked, lost for ideas, or don't know about
how to proceed, brainstorm. Set the timer for three minutes, or
longer, and mind map your way to success by generating a
range of possible solutions. Intensify the impact by encouraging supportive others to brainstorm ideas too.

Ask open generative questions to increase your range of
options, "*how, what, where, what else*" etc., and combine
different ideas to open your mind to new ideas and
possibilities.

Don't close down any 'crazy' ideas prematurely.

*I don't want to be seen as an outsider necessarily, but it means I
can carry on with experimentation
and innovation.*

~ Dame Zaha Mohammad Hadid, architect

FANTASIA

Science is the observation of things possible, whether present or past. Prescience is the knowledge of things that may come to pass, though but slowly.

~ Leonardo da Vinci

What do you ask first? What's realistic? Or what's possible? So many people want guarantees of success before taking action. But Leonardo's success was primarily driven by his deep and fertile imagination—or what he termed *fantasia*. Fantasia he believed, was a core requirement for a successful creator.

He fed his imagination with a diversity of sources. Records kept from his book lists showed that he owned chivalric romances, imaginative poetry, collections of tales, fables and jests, as well, as scientific and fact-based texts.

To succeed, you need to establish a union between *the*

intelletto, rational understanding, and *fantasia*, imaginative composition.

But in the beginning give yourself permission to let your mind, and spirit soar. Don't get bogged down by limited rational thinking. This will stifle creativity, and narrow your capacity for out-of-the-orbit thinking.

Numerous scientific studies show that novelty and 'weird' experiences stimulate creativity. Imagine, as Leonardo did, impossible things. Daydream. Create or read about absurd things.

Your Challenge

How can you create more fantastical ideas?

What's impossible? What if it were possible? How could you make it come true? How would your future be different?

Believe in the fantastic.

~ Dame Zaha Mohammad Hadid, architect

LEAD DON'T FOLLOW

Once you have tasted flight, you will forever walk the earth with your eyes turned skyward, for there you have been, and there you will always long to return.

~ Leonardo da Vinci

L eonardo combined what he loved with his vision and talent for fulfilling future needs. The threat of war made him design things that would protect cities. The desire for faster travel propelled his quest to find a way for man to fly. Illness and death drove him to understand the human body.

He once said, "The painter will produce pictures of little merit if he takes the works of others as his standard."

His creations were original, and many artists of the time copied him—including Raphael. Many of Leonardo's designs were spectacularly ahead of his time.

So many of his ideas were impossible to build during the 15th and 16th centuries with the tools available and Leonardo's financial constraints. However 500-plus years later he's still regarded as a leader.

Your Challenge

Don't chase the market. Create a need, or fulfil anticipated ones. Don't be deterred if at first you don't succeed. Do what you dream about and wait for the world to catch up. No one really knows what, or who, be the next hot thing.

Persevere with your vision. Let the beauty and imagineering you love be the work that you do. Cocoon yourself in the protective magic and power of creative, lateral, blue-skies thinking.

Read and learn about other leaders and pioneers. And become the lead character in your own book of life.

You are the storyteller of your own life, and you can create your own legend, or not.

~ Isabel Allende, author

PUT YOUR WEIGHT INTO YOUR DREAMS

A man will always, involuntarily, throw the greater weight towards the point whither he desires to move than in any other direction.

~ Leonardo da Vinci

It's pretty hard to gain any traction when your heart is not engaged. Whether you're just starting out on your quest for success, or facing a mountain of obstacles, it's imperative to put your weight into your dreams.

Leonardo threw his mind, body and soul into his deepest desires. When he became obsessed with mathematics and sacred geometry this became his focus, with some people complaining he had stopped painting and 'had little time for the brush.'

When understanding the human body became central the weight of his considerable mind was channeled into figuring out its workings.

When you truly commit, mind, body and soul you'll engage the laws of physics and move forwards with incredible velocity.

Your Challenge

How whole-hearted are you?

Do you have one foot in the door and the other foot out?

What would it take to strengthen your desire?

Put your weight into your dreams but keep an eye on the day-to-day realities that sustain you.

*The biggest adventure you can take
is to live the life of your dreams.*

~ Oprah, businesswoman

FOCUS

The mind that engages in subjects of too great variety becomes confused and weakened.

~ Leonardo da Vinci

There are divergent thoughts on what it means to be focused. Some people believe you focus on only one thing, one task, one priority at the time. Only when you have finished that task do you move to the next. Great! If that works for you, you have your success strategy.

But some people like Leonardo da Vinci thrive on variety. Seeing one thing through to the end often bored him—stifling his creativity and productivity.

Leonardo also disproves the myth that you can't have more than one passion to be successful. He was passionate about so many things—beauty, nature, science, human behaviour, nature, architecture, the human body, sacred geometry, the soul…and more.

However look closely and you'll see a central unifying theme—the attempt to replicate nature's beauty and power, and the acquisition of knowledge born from his own experience.

He described himself as many things, but tellingly he once said he was simply an inventor. He acquired knowledge to see what more he could do with it.

Your Challenge

If a lack of focus is something getting in your way, really drill down into the causal factors. Play the role of scientist. Discover the cause, identify the effect, hypothesise solutions, and experiment until you find a strategy that works. Perhaps the issue is less about focus and more about self-discipline!

Eckhart Tole, author of *The Power of Now*, advocates surrender. Whatever is holding your attention now—surrender to it. Focus on what you 'should' be doing at a later date

Juggling too many balls? Prioritise them, set a timer, and allocate segmented time for all the competing activities you feel must get done.

Practise creative procrastination. Ask yourself, "What is the best use of my time right now?" Put off everything else.

Remind yourself of a time when you struggled to focus. What worked then that you could apply now?

The Universe has a wonderful way of self-correcting once you get out of your own way.

In our daily lives, moving from struggle to grace requires practice and commitment.

~ Arianna Huffington, businesswoman

TAKE ACTION

It had long since come to my attention that people of accomplishment rarely sat back and let things happen to them. They went out and happened to things.

~ Leonardo da Vinci

Do you have an action, 'make things happen' mindset, or do you believe in luck, serendipity, going with the flow, or waiting for opportunities to find you?

So many people take a passive route when it comes to achieving their goals. Others wait until all the stars are aligned. Not Leonardo, and hopefully not you!

Despite being criticised for not finishing everything he started, when Leonardo wanted to achieve something, he visualised the end goal, and did what he needed to do to make his vision a reality.

When Leonardo needed a new patron—one with power and

deep pockets—he didn't sit back. Sometimes he faked it until he made it by talking up his successes.

When he 'cold-called' Ludovico Sforza, the then de facto ruler of Milan, seeking employment he talked-up his achievements.

Fully aware that Sforza was looking to employ military engineers, Leonardo drafted an application letter emphasising engineering talents and skills he had yet to fully develop, and assuring the Duke of his ability to achieve impossible feats.

Leonardo got the job!

Your Challenge

Do you plan your life by:

- Beginning with the end in mind—planning at least five to ten years ahead, and working back from there to ensure that everything you do now moves you ahead?
- Creating outcome-focused goals?
- Or do you get bogged down in rigidly planning every minute step you have to make to achieve the changes —instead of trusting you will figure it, or trusting the Universe or providence to deliver?

It's a balancing act! Whatever your approach, pledge to make your success a reality. Act as if who and what you desire to be is already a reality.

Luck is preparation meeting opportunity.

~ Oprah, businesswoman

GROUND YOUR VISION

The earth has a spirit of growth.

~ Leonardo da Vinci

Leonardo's visions came from the skies and realms above; the implementation of his ideas from the earth below. To achieve success he knew he needed to ground himself. He new he had to come from a place of earthy strength and stillness.

Sometimes during the visionary process your mind may race, as Leonardo's did, with wild, unbridled excitement about all the possibilities. Or perhaps, your mind may drum with anxiety. Unstructured energy can pull you in different directions, over-whelming or immobilising you.

Ground your vision and prepare to engage your analytical mind, you'll have better judgement, clarity of thinking and more self-assured energy.

Your Challenge

Reorganise yourself. Touch base with what's real., what's practical, what needs to be done. Ground your vision by identifying the body of work you'll need to complete to make your ideas tangible.

Defrag your visionary mind. Take your shoes off and connect with the earth. Step away from technology. Spend time quietly in nature, as Leonardo often did, listen to Her whispers. Notebook in hand, allow your intuition to guide you.

When you're feeling grounded set about gathering and analysing information, designing and testing solutions to problems, and formulating plans. This can still be done creatively.

For example, you may wish to:

- Name all the tangible seeds you need to plant
- Identify the optimal planting conditions that will allow your ideas to sprout
- Weed out any inner blocks, limiting beliefs, assumptions or mind-chatter that may keep you from taking positive action.
- Prepare your planting plan
- Go plant!

If you're a list maker—you know what to do!

Facilitate the translation of principles
into explicit practical forms.

~ Ada Lovelace, mathematician

PRINCIPLE FOUR: EMPOWER YOUR SPIRIT

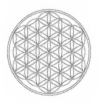

WORSHIP THE GOD WITHIN

The definition of the soul I leave to the imaginations of friars, those fathers of the people who know all secrets by inspiration. I leave alone the sacred books; for they are supreme truth.

~ Leonardo da Vinci

Rumours abound about Leonardo's beliefs, but one thing is certain, he was not blind to the failings, corruption and hypocrisy of the men who claimed to represent God on earth.

The Medici and Borgias, members of the ruling classes during the Renaissance, rose to be clerics and popes. Historical records confirm they were motivated by their own pursuit of power and pleasure more than the salvation of others.

They also actively censored the cultivation of beliefs which threatened their own power base.

Leonardo was also aware of men altering and rewriting ancient biblical texts—including the zealous Dominican priest Savonarola, who also burned thousands of beautiful artworks and musical instruments he regarded as sinful vanities.

But spirituality and faith, as it is for so many people, was important to Leonardo's success. Not just because so many of his commissions were from the church, but because he believed in the power of God, divinity and soul.

Rather than subscribe to dogma Leonardo found his strength and grounded his faith in roots that can be traced to ancient Gnosticism and Neoplatonism.

Gnostic ideas influenced many ancient religions and believed that gnosis—interpreted as knowledge, enlightenment 'oneness with God, the divine creator—could be accessed directly. Searching for wisdom by helpful others led to direct communion with God—no third party intermediary such as a pope or priest required.

Many of Leonardo's Christian-based religious paintings are said to 'hide in plain sight' Leonardo's deepest beliefs, and rebellious thinking, which if more strongly asserted would have been called heresy.

Deepak Chopra writes in *The Seven Spiritual Laws of Success*, once you learn to live in harmony with natural law, a sense of well-being, good health, fulfilling relationships, energy and enthusiasm for life and material abundance will spring forth easily and effortlessly.

Some of many benefits Leonardo gained from worshipping the god within include:

- Access to divine wisdom
- A deep connection with universal knowledge

- Faith, hope and strength during testing times
- A guiding sense of purpose

Your Challenge

What does spirituality mean to you?

What spiritual beliefs and practices sustain and empower you?

If spirituality is not something you believe in examine your beliefs. Why? Why not? What mistaken beliefs might you have absorbed?

While many people have found comfort in religion, others have had traumatic experiences. Examine how religion and spirituality are the same and how they differ.

He who has a mind to understand,
let him understand.

~ Mary Magdalene, in The Gospel of Mary

BE AN OUTLIER

*I awoke, only to find the rest
of the world was still asleep.*

~ Leonardo da Vinci

Too often people are afraid to stand out from the crowd. Often the innovative path is the path less followed but, as actress Drew Barrymore says, "Originality is believing in your individuality, believing in yourself, and being willing to take risks, even though people might think you're weird for doing it."

Yet so many people seek, and then struggle, to fit in with the 'norm.' But not Leonardo da Vinci—he was one of the greatest and most successful outliers of all.

He was a free-thinker, unbounded by convention. He was motivated by his own search for truth born from his own experience—not the dogma of others.

So many people are sleeping through their lives. Leonardo was awake, shining the light on truth, advancement, the progress of humanity.

Only in recent years have engineers begun to construct his amazing designs. Were it not for his curiosity and willingness to stand out from the crowd Leonardo da Vinci would have faded into obscurity.

Your Challenge

Are you prepared to stand out from the crowd and live a significant life?

What do you need to start, stop, do more of, and less of to be a confident outlier?

I don't really feel I'm part of the establishment. I'm not outside, I'm on the kind of edge, I'm dangling there. I quite like it ... I'm not against the establishment per se. I just do what I do and that's it.

~ Dame Zaha Mohammad Hadid, architect

DEVOTE YOURSELF

A life without love, is no life at all.

~ Leonardo da Vinci

S uccess without love is no success at all. A life dedicated to what inspires you, that fills you with joy and gives you passion and fulfilment is a life truly lived. The French call this your *métier*.

Others, like author Deepak Chopra call this your dharma, or purpose in life. Joy, bliss—call it what you will—you'll know it when you feel it.

On my business card I have the following quote by the ancient philosopher Sophocles, "One word frees us from the weight and pain of life: That word is love."

Love is such a power antidote to all that troubles us—it's the Swiss Army knife of all things healing. My passion, purpose, and inspiration is simple—love. I love to bring more love into the world. I know that love is a contagious energy—when I am inspired my love spreads love into the world.

Leonardo's inspiration? Nature. He sought to both understand and replicate Her beauty and her wisdom—and in doing so, to bring more love into existence.

Love is the highest, most powerful vibration on earth. It radiates light, driving out darkness. When you work with love people feel it. It permeates everything you do and draws people who are attracted by the power of this energy to you.

Your Challenge

Wed yourself to the experiences that awaken your heart. What or who do you love with such a passion you will devote your life to it?

Heart is what drives us and determines our fate.

~ Isabel Allende, author

FOLLOW your passion and purpose to prosperity—online coaching program

To find and live your life purpose you may prefer to watch inspirational and practical videos and other strategies to help you to fulfil your potential.

Click here to enrol or find out more—the-coaching-lab. teachable.com/p/follow-your-passion-and-purpose-to-prosperity

INTEGRATE YOUR MIND, BODY AND SOUL

All knowledge has its origins in our perceptions.

~ Leonardo da Vinci

Thinking and feeling, heart versus head, mind versus body, have played a dual battle for supremacy throughout history as the centre for knowledge.

Yet in truth neither is supreme. The power you give to one over the other is only in your perceptions.

However, many people believe that love, awe, wonder, worship —and success, in particular—depends on the integration of your mind, body and soul. For balance, all must work as one.

Leonardo was fascinated with how the heart functioned, but also the pineal gland, a small structure about the size of a pea, located in the middle of the brain.

He believed, as René Descartes, a French philosopher, mathematician, and scientist, that the pineal gland was where the soul attached to the body and passion resided. Accessing this tiny gland, he and other modern-day scientists believe, provides a direct channel to higher wisdom and divine intelligence.

Perhaps this was how Leonardo was able to so accurately predict the future.

Your Challenge

Access this higher knowledge by adopting some of the following spiritual practices:

- Meditating
- Journaling
- Following your passions
- Surrounding yourself with like-minded people
- Immersing yourself in nature
- Accessing your sub-conscious and super-conscious minds
- Retreating into solitude
- Reading sacred books and accessing ancients' knowledge of the spiritual realms
- Consulting the Akashic Records, or "Hall of Knowledge. (I invite you to contact me for a personalised reading).

Honour the mind-body and spiritual dimension. When your spirit is off-centre, the odds are your work and relationships will be too.

O admirable necessity!

O powerful action!
What mind can penetrate your nature?
What language can express this marvel?
None, to be sure.
This is where human discourse
turns toward the contemplation of the divine.

~ Leonardo da Vinci

WORK WITH SPIRIT

Where the spirit does not work with the hand, there is no art.

~ Leonardo da Vinci

I f your soul is not in your work, there is no heart. Without heart your work lacks passion, purpose and power.

These are all sources of energy and the key to the authenticity people love. People can spot a fake. Fakes and frauds lack conviction, energy and vitality.

Oprah once said, "I am not successful because of luck. I am successful because I paid attention." She also said, "I wish I'd known be authentic would make me so much money."

Discovering, honouring and sharing your gifts and working with your soul purpose is to work with spirit.

Your Challenge

Pay attention to what fills your soul with fire.

Pay attention to what's real for you.

Pay attention when your spirit feels suffocated.

Whatever you put your hand to, imbue it with the spirit of love.

Passion is energy. Feel the power that comes from focusing on what excites you. You know you are on the road to success if you would do your job, and not be paid for it.

~ Oprah, businesswoman

SHOW UP

I have been impressed with the urgency of doing. Knowing is not enough: we must apply. Being willing is not enough; we must do.

~ Leonardo da Vinci

To be inspired is to be in spirit, and inspiration has to find you working or it won't come out to play. Eighty percent of success is empowering your mind, body and spirit by showing up.

Showing up requires the ability to balance creativity with flexibility and discipline.

To be disciplined is to be committed, devoted, able to control your Self in accordance with, and sometimes against, your desires.

You may be a genius, gifted or have an IQ of 160, but if you lack self-discipline and follow through your success will be limited.

Leonardo affirmed the importance of this by writing reminders to himself of the superiority of doing to knowing. Like two very gifted dance partners, one must lead.

Your Challenge

How can you create a sense of urgency and show up?

What do you need to start, stop, do more of or less of?

Show up. Show up.
When you show up the muse shows up, too.

~ Isabel Allende, author

FIND YOUR SACRED SPACE

Men of lofty genius when they are doing the least work are most active.

~ Leonardo da Vinci

Finding your sacred space—a place where you can retreat from the world, contemplate, and reflect, and just take time out from your overloaded conscious mind, is an important part of connecting with your higher self and inner wisdom.

Being in nature was one of Leonardo's favourite sacred spaces. Perhaps it's yours too. Maybe your sacred space is a favourite room, a garden shed or some other place where you can have uninterrupted time.

Your sacred space may be amongst other like-minded people, perhaps a spiritual place of worship or a meditation retreat. Or even a place where you can indulge your passions and joys. Doing something you love is often a meditation in itself.

Resist setting an agenda or specific expectations. Go with nothing more than to dedicate yourself to nurturing the divine within. Nourish your soul and watch your spirit and capacity for greatness soar.

Your Challenge

Where is your sacred space?

If you don't have one make finding it a priority.

My bedroom is my sanctuary. It's like a refuge, and it's where I do a fair amount of designing —at least conceptually, if not literally.

~ Vera Wang, fashion designer

THE SACREDNESS OF NUMBERS

No human investigation can be called real science if it cannot be demonstrated mathematically.

~ Leonardo Da Vinci

You may believe in lucky numbers or you may call it superstition but Leonardo revered the science and sacred mysteries of mathematical proportion.

His curiosity piqued he devoted many years to understanding and applying the ancient knowledge of sacred geometry.

Why sacred? Sacred geometry involves sacred universal patterns which appear and are used in the design in *everything* in our reality.

The whole of the Universe is said to be contained within a grain of sand. The mysteries of science, mathematics and the higher heavens can be found in naturally recurring patterns of numbers which link man, animals, nature and the Universe.

Guided by the sacredness of numbers and divine proportion some of the world's most enduring sacred monuments dedicated to worship, beauty, and excellence have been created—including Egypt's Great Pyramids, and Florence's magnificent Cathedral of *Santa Maria del Fiore*.

Geometry and mathematical ratios, harmonics and proportions are also found in some of the world's most captivating art works, including Leonardo's Last Supper and the Mona Lisa. They're also found in light, cosmology and music.

So powerful are these forms, they are believed by many to enable you to commune directly with The Divine (God or Source), rather than requiring intermediaries such as a priest.

Coco Chanel, (the inspiration for the second book in *The Art of Success* series), believed so strongly in the power of the number five she named her perfume Chanel No5.

Taught the precepts of theosophy by one of her lovers, she knew the numerological significance of it, as representative of the fifth element—the legendary *quinta essentia* of the alchemists, the Classical quintessence of which it is believed by many the cosmos is made.

"I'm presenting my dress collection on the 5th of May, the fifth month of the year," she once said.

Your Challenge

What numbers are harmonious to you?

What are your success numbers?

Look deeper into the world of numbers and proportion and discover their secret mysteries.

If you find from your own experience that something is a fact and it contradicts what some authority has written down, then you must abandon the authority and base your reasoning on your own findings.

~ Leonardo da Vinci

PRINCIPLE FIVE: EMPOWER YOUR MIND

CULTIVATE A SUCCESS MINDSET

You cannot help being good,
because your hand and your mind,
being accustomed to gather flowers
would ill know how to pluck thorns.

~ Leonardo da Vinci

His Holiness the 14th Dalai Lama once said, "Negative thoughts are like weeds, but positive thoughts are like flowers—they need nurturing every day."

Leonardo proactively fertilised his mind, and empowered his resolve by focusing on his dreams, goals and aspirations.

To steady himself against self-doubt or the attacks of others he actively cultivated a success mindset by using affirmations, journaling, meditating, channeling and accessing the spiritual realms, and surrounding himself with like-minded, aspirational and inspirational people.

If you actively cultivate a success mindset you cannot help being good, because your mind, focused on the fruits of your positive intention and effort will act as a barrier to discouragement, keeping away the thorns of self-doubt, procrastination, fear or any of the other things toxic to your success.

Your Challenge

Attitude is everything. How can you cultivate a success mindset?

Think like a queen. A queen is not afraid to fail. Failure is another stepping stone to greatness.

~ Oprah, businesswoman

MOTIVATE YOURSELF

You will never have a greater or lesser dominion than that over yourself...the height of a man's success is gauged by his self-mastery; the depth of his failure by his self-abandonment.

~ Leonardo da Vinci

To succeed in life you need to master yourself, assume the command position, take control and motivate yourself. Whether you need to master new technical skills or master the art of self-discipline, when you fail to be the boss of you, you are giving away your power.

Leonardo once said that people were more motivated by fear than they were love. Desperation can be a wonderful motivator. But so can love.

Whether you're fuelled by the carrot or the whip your job is to produce your work to a special level, in a specific amount of time, in order to create the life you desire. No excuses.

Whether your motivation is intrinsic—the rewards that come from doing the work itself; or extrinsic—external rewards such as money or status, the questions you ask can be powerful catalysts to inspired action. The art lies in crafting questions that get better outcomes.

Your Challenge

Instead of saying, "How can I be more self-disciplined?" asking, "How can I master the art of self-motivation and discipline and have fun doing it?" may yield better results.

Similarly, instead of saying, "How can I be more successful?" try asking "How can I be more successful and have a blast doing it?" Listen for the answers and then take action.

Stephen Covey, author of *The 7 Habits of Highly Effective People*, says the ability to subordinate an impulse to a value is the essence of the proactive person.

What do you value? Fulfilment? Freedom? Joy? Continuous learning? Achieving a worthwhile goal? High earnings? Achieving your potential? Completion? Or something else? Often the things you struggle against reveal your values most

Reaffirm your success values to empower your success.

Where there is no struggle,
there is no strength.

~ Oprah, businesswoman

OVERCOME PROCRASTINATION

Inaction saps the vigours of the mind.

~ Leonardo da Vinci

L eonardo once wrote in his journal, "It is easier to resist at the beginning than at the end."

This simple statement is a reminder of what we all know to be true— getting started is often the most difficult part of taking inspired action.

The result is almost always procrastination—the great robber of time, talent and potential.

But it's an easy thief to tame if you keep your mind focused on your end goal and just do it. Once you get started your mind and spirit will become instantly invigorated.

Your Challenge

Do you want success badly enough to just do the things that need to be done—NOW?

What disempowering beliefs, attitudes or habits are holding you back? Dig deep. Unearth the culprits.

Recall a time in the past when you procrastinated. What was your success strategy?

Whip procrastination into shape by taking inspired action. Set the timer for five minutes and see how much harder it is to stop once you've started.

I made a conscious decision not to stop.

~ Dame Zaha Mohammad Hadid, architect

CULTIVATE HOPE

One's thoughts turn towards Hope.

~ Leonardo da Vinci

Common obstacles to success include fear, self-doubt, anxiety, and other crippling thoughts. But what if all you had to do to tame these uglies was cultivate hope?

The power of hope is grounded firmly in spiritual and religious practices but also in science. Like the ancient Greeks and Romans, Leonardo da Vinci, and even 18th century physicians, recognised the physiological effects of mind-power and hope on the body.

Successful medical outcomes, even when the intervention is a placebo, further evidence the impact of maintaining a positive expectation.

If like me, you've manifested miracles in your own life, by

maintaining a positive expectation, you'll know the power of hope.

Thoughts *do* become things. Scientists Gregg Braden and also Bruce Lipton, author of *The Biology of Belief,* have evidenced this.

But hope can only flourish when you believe that what you do can make a difference, that you recognise that you have choices, and that your actions can create a future which differs from your present situation.

When you empower your belief in your ability to gain some control over your circumstances, you are no longer entirely at the mercy of forces outside yourself. You are back in the driving seat.

What you believe has a tremendous influence on the likelihood of success. Reframe your fears and buoy your dreams with hope. Not, "I'm afraid of failing" but "I hope to succeed," or something similar.

Your Challenge

How could you cultivate more hope?

Fearlessness is like a muscle.
I know from my own life
that the more I exercise it
the more natural it becomes
to not let my fears run me.

~ Arianna Huffington, businesswomen

ALLOW NO DOUBT

Obstacles cannot crush me;
every obstacle yields to stern resolve.

~ Leonardo da Vinci

Attitude is everything. Be a guard for your words, thoughts and feelings. Don't let self-doubt be the thing that deflates you.

Winners like Leonardo da Vinci are too busy to be sad, too positive to be doubtful, too optimistic to be fearful, too focused on success and too determined to be defeated.

Be your biggest fan. Back yourself 100 percent. We all have doubts, but it's amazing how your doubts will disappear once you're doing the things you love.

As you've already read, Leonardo cultivated hope, visualised the end goal, used affirmations, and studious effort to slay his doubt demons.

He also backed his ideas and saw failure as a normal and often necessary part of success.

Your Challenge

Are you your biggest fan or worst enemy? How can you stay positive, confident and optimistic?

You will need the confidence to take new steps every time; hard work will give you that layer of confidence.

~ Dame Zaha Mohammad Hadid, architect

DON'T LET THE CRITICS STOP YOU

The greatest deception men suffer
is from their own opinions.

~ Leonardo da Vinci

L istening too much to others, or overly seeking validation and approval, can really hinder your success. If you try to please everyone you'll never succeed.

Plenty of successful people have received scathing reviews, rejections and public humiliation from peers and critics but they persevered with their vision anyway.

You'll know some of the more famous ones. Author J.K Rowling's *Harry Potter* series was rejected many times by publishers who told her that there wasn't a big market for books targeted at children.

The singer Meatloaf was told that he was too fat to make it big and no one would want to see a 'weird' performance like *Bat*

Out of Hell.

Film producer Peter Jackson was cautioned to stay away from a trilogy and make *The Lord of the Rings* into one normal length movie.

Yet these men and women, and others like them, stayed true to their quest. And they all went on to be colossal successes.

Other people may believe their criticisms of you, your ideas, your work. But what if they are wrong? What if your vision, like Leonardo Da Vinci's was back in the 1500's, is way ahead of its time?

Sometimes feedback is helpful. But not if it stops you in your tracks or you are so consumed with garnering everyone's approval you become immobilised.

Nobody can stop you but you. You have to ignore your harshest critics. To thy self you must remain true. Imagine how many of Leonardo's ideas would never have come to fruition if he'd listened to others.

Your Challenge

Forge ahead. Blaze your road to success with your victories— even if the victory is just the one you win over your self-doubt, your laziness, your procrastination, your thoughts that you have no talent, or some other self-defeating chatter.

What's worse—the disappointment of criticism and bad reviews, or the bitter, bitter disappointment of a life spent unfulfilled and filled with regret?

All life arises out of choice. What choices are you making now?

How can you stay strong in the wake of criticism?

How can you do more of what's working for you, and less of what's not? What can you start and stop doing to boost your chances of success?

No one ever truly knows what the market will do next, nor the music you hold inside!

TOO MANY PEOPLE die with regret . . . far better to say at least you tried . . . and even better, that you kept going. Trust yourself and believe in your work!

It's not 'What do I want to do?'
It's 'What kind of life do I want to have?'

~ Arianna Huffington, businesswoman

MAINTAIN SOME BALANCE

Every now and then go away, have a little relaxation, for when you come back to your work your judgment will be surer. Go some distance away because then the work appears smaller and more of it can be taken in at a glance and a lack of harmony and proportion is more readily seen.

~ Leonardo da Vinci

Workaholism is an addiction for many passionate people. Others use overwork to medicate their unhappiness in other areas of their life—most commonly dissatisfaction with their relationships.

When you work slavishly, particularly at something you love, your brain releases chemicals called opiates which create feelings of euphoria. No wonder it's hard to step away!

Euphoria stems from the Greek word *euphoria*—the power of enduring easily. But consider what the state of endurance implies. Enduring implies force or strain, or gritting your teeth and bearing it at times. Force or strain with no respite leads to stress, robbing you of vital energy.

Many people find when they don't step away from their work they suffer disillusionment, and things that once filled them with passion no longer fill them with joy. Resentment builds and relationships with family, friends etc. can suffer.

Addictively working offers a short-term fix, but lasting happiness needs variety—and nourishment. Being with family or friends, engaging in a hobby, spending time in nature, learning something new, helping others, or just being solitary will help you avoid burnout, nourish your brain, heart and soul, improve your judgement and restore harmony.

To be truly happy and successful you must be able to be at peace when you are working and when you are at rest.

Leonardo would often take breaks from his work to refresh his mind and spirit. While others claimed he took too long to finish things he knew the importance of replenishing his focus to maintain a clear perspective.

He also valued sleep, noting in one of his journals that some of his best insights came when his mind was not working.

Even if you love the work that you do it is fun to get away from it and have objective-free time, space to unwind and reset yourself. When you return your focus will be surer, your vision refreshed and your confidence larger.

Your Challenge

Who are you when you are not working? Do you still feel successful? Worthy?

When was the last time you truly relaxed?

Can you think of a time when you stepped away from your work and when you returned, your mind was clearer, your judgement surer?

Schedule time out—and be firm with yourself. Stay away from anything that feeds your addiction!

What can you start doing, stop doing, do more of, and less of? What are all the benefits that will flow?

By helping us keep the world in perspective, sleep gives us a chance to refocus on the essence of who we are. And in that place of connection, it is easier for the fears and concerns of the world to drop away.

~ Arianna Huffington, businesswoman

LEARN YOUR WAY TO SUCCESS

Learning never exhausts the mind.

~ Leonardo da Vinci

L eonardo was curious about everything. Once he'd understood one thing his mind went in search of new knowledge. Perhaps this is the secret to his longevity. He lived until he was 67, at a time when the life-expectancy was only 39.7 years. And in death he achieved immortality.

Feeling tired? Bored? Fatigued? Try a FTE—first time experience. What have you always wanted to know or learn but never thought you could?

You may surprise yourself and in the process discover a new path to success. Sometimes the best way to reset your life, gain new knowledge, or master a new skill is to gain inspiration from others.

Tim Ferris, an American author, entrepreneur, angel investor, and public speaker, recently shared how creating his podcast, *The Tim Ferris Show*, was his way of taking a break from the stress of his other professional endeavours.

While there was a lot to learn, he was determined to have fun. What started out as a side-gig has now become a phenomenal success. Best of all he says he's always learning new things and being continually inspired.

Your Challenge

Stay curious. Put your heart, mind and soul into acquiring new knowledge.

Be patient. Enjoy not knowing. It takes time to acquire mastery.

Anyone can be good, but being awesome takes practice—are you willing to put in 10,000 hours to achieve mastery?

Whether you succeed or not is irrelevant, there is no such thing. Making your unknown known is the important thing—and keeping the unknown always beyond you.

~ Georgia O'Keeffe, artist

PLAY

I love those who can smile in trouble.

~ Leonardo da Vinci

Did you know that at the age of four, 96 percent of children think they can be anything they want to be, but that by the age of 18 only four percent of them still believe it?

As we grow up and get sensible, we tend to close down our sense of possibility, trading in our dreams and passions for a steady pay check and a "proper job". Somewhere along the way we have lost the ability to play. Playing can seem irresponsible to many people.

But Leonardo da Vinci recognised and embraced the value of play, as did Albert Einstein many years later when he said, "Creativity is intelligence having fun."

Be playful. Cultivate your inner child. Don't take yourself too seriously. Act up a little, goof-off, experiment—if you find yourself in trouble, smile.

Laughter triggers the release of endorphins, the brain's feel good chemicals, setting off an emotional reaction which makes us feel great.

Benefits of play include:

- Boosting your creativity and problem solving skills
- Reducing stress, anxiety, and depression
- Improving your relationships and connections with others
- Bringing more balance, fun, lightness and levity into your life
- Diminishing your worries
- Increasing your ability to do creative and productive work.

LEONARDO WAS A GREAT PRANKSTER, and he loved surrounding himself with other pranksters—people who were young in mind, body and spirit.

This probably explains why he took in a young 10-year-old apprentice who he nicknamed Salai, *The Devil*. He often wrote in his journal how mischievous and naughty, but also how interesting, the young boy was.

Examples of Leonardo's playful creations include the sets for theatrical productions he designed and stages for his wealthy grown-up patrons, including the Duke of Milan and the King of France.

With his playful approach to experimentation and a positive, joyous response to the world around him, Leonardo da Vinci was a dedicated practitioner of his art, working constantly through his life and producing a very large and varied body of work.

As play researcher and psychiatrist Stuart Brown says in his book *Play: How it Shapes the Brain, Opens the Imagination, and Invigorates the Soul*, "A lack of play should be treated like malnutrition: it's a health risk to your body and mind."

Your Challenge

How can you be more playful—at home and at work?

What benefits will flow?

A well-composed book is a magic carpet
on which we are wafted to a world
that we cannot enter in any other way.

~ Caroline Gordon, novelist

CHASE THE LIGHT

*Darkness steeps everything with its hue, and the more an object is
divided from darkness the more it shows its true and natural
colour.*

~ Leonardo da Vinci

What's your default position when things go awry,
obstacles challenge your resolve, technology goes
belly-up or unforeseen demands on your time derail your
plans?

Does your mood darken? Setbacks are normal foes you'll meet
on the path to success, but how you greet them will determine
the outcome.

Keep your thoughts light. You may need to bring out the big
guns to wage war against doubt, despair and other dark, heavy
thoughts. While they're often part of the journey to success,
you will need to slay them to stay motivated and optimistic.

Leonardo would turn again and again toward the things that created light. He didn't ignore the shadows, but he didn't allow his palette to be overloaded by darkness.

Acceptance, optimism, willpower, grit, stubborn determination and a resolve to persevere are critical skills to cultivate, as is flexibility and the willingness to adapt. Sometimes it's all too hard and you need to hibernate. You can take a lesson from nature in this regard.

Your Challenge

Resist complaining and victim talk—it increases toxicity in your mind and body, hampering your progress.

Throw your energy into positivity—strive to engineer and implement solutions, no matter how small.

Ask for help if too much darkness creeps in.

Peer into the darkness and look for the gift

How can you move from darkness towards the light?

Having to fight hard has made me a better architect.

~ Dame Zaha Mohammad Hadid, architect

LEARN FROM FAILURE

I do not depart from my furrow.

~ Leonardo da Vinci

Although Leonardo is widely recognised as one of the world's greatest geniuses, he also made colossal mistakes and suffered staggering failures which would have felled many.

But he persevered anyway. He knew that learning from his own experience also meant learning from his mistakes.

Experimenting with new painting techniques ruined his fresco, *The Battle of Anghiari,* and nearly destroyed *The Last Supper.* His flying machines never got off the ground, and his attempts to divert the Arno River in Florence was a massive public failure.

But he didn't hang up his artist's apron, nor his inventor's cap. He never strayed from his course—he learned from his failures, accepted them as par for the course, hunkered down and continued his quest to learn, experiment and explore.

The furrow he wished to plough was first-hand experience and experimentation—in this path he succeeded.

Reframe failure. The greatest lessons come not from your successes but from your failures. What can you let your failures teach you? Don't look at hurdles as a negative thing but as a reflective tool on how to improve.

Reading biographies of people like Leonardo da Vinci and other people whose success you admire can give you great encouragement along your path to creating your own victories.

Your Challenge

Are you prepared to fail in order to succeed?

Do you give yourself permission to learn from mistakes? What is the biggest mistake you ever made and what did you learn?

What new experiences are you prepared to embark on?

What would you do differently if you had no fear of making mistakes?

Whose failure story inspires you? Why? What does it teach you?

I have a lot of things to prove to myself. One is that I can live my life fearlessly.

~ Oprah, businesswoman

PRINCIPLE SIX: EMPOWER YOUR BODY

KEEP YOUR BODY HEALTHY

Good judgement proceeds from clear understanding, and a clear understanding comes from reason derived from sound rules, and sound rules are the daughters of sound experience—the common mother of all the sciences and arts.

~ Leonardo da Vinci

It's tougher to succeed if you lack energy, feel stressed, sluggish, lethargic or unhealthy. Artificially stimulating your mind, body and soul won't cut it in the long term.

Strong agile minds and souls need strong agile bodies to carry them. Leonardo's physical strength, but also his grace and agility was well documented.

Giorgio Vasari, a 16th century historian and architect once wrote, "his great strength could restrain the most violent fury, and he could bend an iron knocker or a horseshoe as if it were lead."

Leonardo's passionate quest to understand human anatomy and extensive knowledge of how the body works made him a "one-stop merchant" in achieving and maintaining ultimate health and well-being.

He was well versed in avoiding extremes—too much sloth made one prone to gluttony, too much activity overwhelmed, and too many vain pleasures taken to extremes were the cause of failure.

Your Challenge

What can you stop, start, do more of or less of, to maintain some balance and keep your body healthy?

Do you listen to your body barometer when it tells you to exercise more and sloth around less?

My clients needed to know how to effectively respond to what their intuition was advising, and how they could learn to heal their lives and assist in healing those around them.

~ Dr Mona Lisa Schulz, neuropsychiatrist

STRESS LESS

He who takes medicine is ill advised.

~ Leonardo da Vinci

L eonardo's mind and body appeared never to be at rest. He accomplished more than any man of his time.

But if you read his journals you'll know he was fully aware of the need to stop, take a break, get some rest, eat well, stay away from negative people, keep his mind positive, exercise, do things he loved, play, spend time in nature, experience the quietness of solitude, and many other stress management techniques we are all encouraged to adopt today.

The fact is that stress and success do not make good lovers. Stress-overload has been described as the disease of our modern society. When you are under too much pressure, take too much on and don't take time out, you tend to live your life on overdrive and on the verge of burnout.

When you're stressed you are less effective, make more mistakes, suffer more and are prone to illness.

Very often people turn to 'medicine'—chemical highs, alcohol, and prescription drugs—to manage the symptoms. But the reality is that these only offer temporary relief, masking symptoms which left unresolved can set fire to everything you've worked so hard to achieve.

Your Challenge

Would you die for your job? Destroy your relationships? Sacrifice your mental health?

What can you start, stop, do more of, and less of to keep your stress levels at a healthy optimum?

If [architecture] doesn't kill you, then you're no good.

~ Dame Zaha Mohammad Hadid, architect (died aged 65)

YOU'LL FIND MORE help to minimise stress and boost resilience in my book, *Stress Less. Love Life More: How to Stop Worrying, Reduce Anxiety, Eliminate Negative Thinking and Find Happiness.*

YOU BOOZE YOU LOSE

Here again many vain pleasures are enjoyed, both by the mind in imagining impossible things, and by the body in taking those pleasures that are often the cause of the failing of life. Extremes are to be avoided.

~ Leonardo da Vinci

Alcohol and success don't make good marriage partners, but they're often fatally attracted.

While there's no evidence that Leonardo was a teetotaller, he was a clever man. Experience would have told him what we all know—too much booze muddles the mind, ignites aggression, reduces responsiveness and ultimately depresses.

It's also hard to quit.

Many successful people limit their drinking or consciously decide not to touch a drop. Keeping their resolve takes extraordinary willpower.

US president Donald Trump doesn't drink. Deepak Chopra gave up drinking, saying "I liked it too much."

Julia Cameron, author of *The Artists Way*, fought her way back from alcoholism. Others like Amy Winehouse devastatingly never made it.

Drink to success? Destroying your career, ruining your relationships, sacrificing your sanity, and taking your life is a massive price to pay to celebrate success.

Benefits of not drinking are many, including:

- Authentic happiness
- Increased memory and mental performance
- Better control of your emotions
- Increased productivity
- Sweeter relationships
- Improved confidence, self-esteem
- Stronger ability to focus on your goals and dreams
- Greater intuition and spiritual intelligence

The choice is ultimately yours. Only you know the benefits alcohol delivers or the toll it exacts.

Your Challenge

Trial sobriety—take the 30 day challenge. Experiment with living an alcohol-free life

Do you need help to moderate or quit drinking? Consider purchasing any of my books in the Mindful Drinking series, including *Mind Your Drink: The Surprising Joy of Sobriety* and *Mind Over Mojitos: Easy Recipes for Happier Hours & a Joy-Filled Life*

I'm proud of people who have the determination and the fearlessness to actually go and face their demons and get better. This is a life or death situation.

~ Eva Mendes, actress

MINDFOOD

To keep in health, this rule is wise: eat only when you want and relish food. Chew thoroughly that it may do you good. Have it well cooked, unspiced and undisguised.

~ Leonardo da Vinci

Leonardo knew how magnificent and clever our bodies are. But for everything to fire optimally you need to fuel it with food geared for performance, and not inhale your meal in a race to the finish.

You are what you feed your stomach—which also feeds your mind. Whether you're a vegetarian as Leonardo was, a meat-eater, gluten-free, or something else, ensure you're putting smart fuel into your body.

Modern nutritionists, and health professionals warn of the perils of over and under eating; not eating fresh, seasonal, organic food; and chewing insufficiently.

Diabetes is on the rise. Obesity is an epidemic. Cholesterol and blood pressure is going through the roof. And stress, depression, anxiety and other mental troubles are all trending upward.

Your gut is also your second brain—a major receptor site of dopamine, a neurotransmitter that helps control the brain's reward and pleasure centres. Dopamine also helps regulate feel good feelings we all need to fuel success.

It also regulates movement—enabling you to not only see the rewards of your efforts, but to take action toward them.

Benefits of healthy eating practices include:

- Increased clarity of thinking
- Healthy body weight
- Increased positive emotions
- Enhanced mental, emotional and physical health
- Improved mood
- More energy and stamina
- Improves goal achievement
- Promotes better sleep
- Improves longevity.

Your Challenge

Consider booking a check-up with a naturopath or nutritionist. You may be surprised how many allergies are impacting your optimum health.

Remember, your stomach doesn't have teeth—take the time to chew and enjoy your food.

Implement some new healthy eating habits. What can you start, stop, eat more of, less of to fuel your success?

If you take care of your mind,
you take care of the world.

~ Arianna Huffington, businesswoman

WATER THERAPY

Water is the driving force in nature.

~ Leonardo da Vinci

Nature was Leonardo's true teacher, and understanding this was key to understanding everything. In particular, he was in awe of the power of water. One of the talents he promoted was his skill as a water engineer.

Later he took his knowledge of hydrodynamics and applied it to the study of blood flow in the heart, noting that lack of blood to the artery which nourishes the heart and surrounding areas caused withering and eventual death.

As blood is to your heart, so water is to your body. Leonardo believed our bodies were machines, designed to run on water and minerals. Because we're made up of 72 percent of water it's vitally important for every important body function.

Insufficient quality water intake, too much coffee or other diuretics, and low consumption of fruit and vegetables can present significant health challenges, robbing your mind and body of energy and vitality.

When you are dehydrated your thoughts can become muddled and you can feel more tired, irritable, demotivated and generally lacklustre. Taken to the extreme, lack of water will cause death.

Your Challenge

Create more energy and drive by flushing toxins from your body as well as increasing your connection with water. Some simple, but effective strategies include:

- Drinking at least eight glasses of purified water a day
- Reducing alcohol and coffee
- Consuming more fruits and vegetables—as close to raw as possible
- Splash water on your face whenever you're feeling overwhelmed. Cold water steps up circulation, making you feel invigorated
- Swimming in the sea or a lake, bathing in hot mineral water—either a natural spring, or by adding Epsom Salts, a mineral compound of magnesium and sulfate, to your bath.

A well-hydrated, relaxed body and mind will function more effectively.

To understand the things that are at our door
is the best preparation for understanding
those that lie beyond.

~ Hypatia of Alexandria, astronomer

MOVE INSIDE OUT

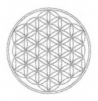

This sun gives spirit and life to plants, and the earth nourishes them with moisture.

~ Leonardo da Vinci

How much time do you spend outside, communing with nature? Research has shown that most of us spend 90 percent of our time indoors, and most of it glued to technology.

Leonardo was born in the hills surrounding Florence and spent much of his time walking in the countryside—boosting his spirits, rejuvenating his mind and nourishing his body with outdoor time.

Vitamin D sufficiency, along with diet and exercise has emerged as one of the most important success factors in human health.

Discipline yourself to go out and get some fresh air—ideally somewhere not too frenzied.

Combine brisk walking with deep breathing to boost your energy levels, short-term memory, and state of mind.

When your breathing is calm and steady your body is in a nurtured state, which helps strengthen your immune system.

Researchers also confirm there is a strong link between breathing, outside energy and beneficial brainwave patterns. Which may explain why so many people say that walking is their meditation—clearing their mind, and allowing space for good ideas to flourish.

Your Challenge

Monitor how much time you spend indoors.

Schedule regular fresh air time.Improve your breathing, and take a brisk walk to increase levels of oxygen.

It was all so far away—there was quiet
and an untouched feel to the country
and I could work as I pleased.

~ Georgia O'Keeffe, artist

NOURISH YOURSELF

If you do not supply nourishment equal to the nourishment that is gone, life will fail in vigour, and if you take away this nourishment, life is entirely destroyed.

~ Leonardo da Vinci

Sometimes pouring all your energy into your work can consume your inspiration and deplete your mojo. Many people mistakenly turn to the medicine cabinet when their energy reserves are depleted, and their mind, body and soul is malnourished.

Leonardo didn't trust doctors. Given his belief in the power of nature it is likely he turned to natural therapies.

Aromatherapy, using the scents of plants and flowers, is one of many ancient remedies validated by modern science. To replenish his weary mind and stimulate new ideas Leonardo would burn a mixture of juniper and sage, inhaling their sweet, restorative scent.

Nourishment can also be provided by being around people who inspire and encourage you, nourish you goals and put vitality back into your soul.

Topping up and fulfilling your body's spiritual needs is too often neglected. To nourish myself I need to meditate, write in my journal, connect with nature, connect with my SELF. Using essential oils and regular massage with energy workers is another one of many ways I nourish my SELF. Reiki and other energy techniques rebalance energy, realign polarities, and nourish the heart.

Your Challenge

What nourishes you?

If you've never tried energy healing do a Leonardo—book a session and let your own experience be your judge.

Investigate the power of smell. Create your own success blend or have an expert create one for you. Beginning with how you want to feel is a good place to start.

Inspirational people are vitamins for the soul. Who can you hang out with? Who do you need to avoid!

What books nourish you?

Holy persons draw to themselves all that is earthly. . . . The earth is at the same time mother.
She is mother of all that is natural, mother of all

that is human. She is the mother of all,
for contained in her are the seeds of all.

~ Hildegard of Bingen, preacher, healer, scientist

SLEEP YOUR WAY TO THE TOP

Time stays long enough for those who use it.

~ Leonardo da Vinci

Many people sacrifice their sleep in the mistaken belief they'll be more productive. But modern science proves conclusively if you skip out on sleep you're compromising not just your efficiency, but also your health.

"We're suffering a sleep crisis," warns Arianna Huffington, the co-founder and editor-in-chief of The Huffington Post, and the author of *The Sleep Revolution: Transforming Your Life One Night at a Time.* The chronic need to be "plugged in" is hurting our health, productivity, relationships and happiness.

A February 2016 study from the US-based Centers for Disease Control and Prevention reported that sleeping less than seven hours a day can lead to an increased risk of obesity, diabetes, high blood pressure, heart disease, stroke and frequent mental distress. None of which will aid your quest for success.

Your Challenge

Try a few of Arianna's tips to help ensure you get a great sleep:

- Meditate for 20 minutes in the morning and at the end of the day to defrag and reconnect with yourself
- Get ready for bed 30 minutes before bedtime
- Turn off all devices and leave them outside your bedroom
- Only read physical books in bed instead of using an e-reader
- End the day with gratitude—write down three things you're grateful for
- Have a hot bath with Epsom Salts
- If you wake in the night meditate
- Be ruthless about prioritising your well-being.

LEONARDO DIDN'T HAVE ELECTRICITY, Facebook, and the gadgets that keep us up at night, but he did know how awesome sleep was. He once asked, "Why does the eye see more clearly when asleep than the imagination when awake?"

Remind yourself of the benefits that will flow while you sleep, and sleep more!

By helping us keep the world in perspective, sleep gives us a chance to refocus on the essence of who we are. And in that place of connection, it is easier for the fears and concerns of the world to drop away.

~ Arianna Huffington, businesswoman

PLANT POWER

I have from an early age abjured the use of meat, and the time will come when men such as I will look upon the murder of animals as they now look upon the murder of men.

~ Leonardo da Vinci

L eonardo was a vegetarian in a culture where killing animals for food and amusement was the norm. *"My body will not be a tomb for other creatures,"* he vowed.

Regardless of Leonardo's motives many people attribute a diet high in vegetables and plant-based proteins and low in meat consumption to their success.

Where once eating meat was associated with strength and power, a growing number of powerful and successful people are embracing the vegetarian or vegan lifestyle.

Former US President Bill Clinton switched to a meat- and

dairy-free diet after a health scare. The low-fat, plant-based diet helped him shed weight and restore his damaged heart.

Many famous Olympians and highly successful athletes are also either vegan, vegetarian or cutting meat from their daily diets. Contrary to what many believe it's possible to succeed in the highly intensive and competitive world of sports without meat.

Your Challenge

Are you motivated to reconsider how you fuel your body?

I'm not advocating that you must become a vegetarian, but you may want to experiment with a change which may accelerate your success.

Experiment. Instead of animal based proteins check out alternative vegetable and other plant-based food proteins. You may want to keep a food, mood and success journal to monitor the changes and results.

As long as I live I will have
control over my being.

~ Artemisia Gentileschi, artist

PRINCIPLE SEVEN: EMPOWER YOUR RELATIONSHIPS

SERVE ONLY ONE MASTER

You cannot serve two masters.

~ Leonardo da Vinci

S ome people fear success because they're afraid succeeding might mean having to choose work over intimate relationships. Others fear abandonment.

One of my clients only found her true groove in life when she left an unhealthy marriage—saving her career and her health in the process. Others have found their success is strengthened by the love and support of their significant other.

Only you can determine what your priorities are, how to balance competing demands on your time and energy and what you may, or not may not, have to sacrifice. What matters most is maintaining a healthy self-esteem.

Healthy self-esteem means that you don't have to be in a relationship to feel love. You will always have the love you feel for yourself and (ideally) the love you feel for your work. You'll also attract love to you—the love and admiration of people who love you for you and for your work.

Your Challenge

What beliefs do you have about success and relationships? How can you challenge these beliefs safely?

Who do you admire that works and lives with healthy self-love, regardless of others' value judgements?

Sometimes, women feel they have to do everything—work, manage the house, look after the children—but there's too much to do. So you have to learn early on that you can't do everything yourself, and you have to learn to trust other people to work on your vision.

~ Dame Zaha Mohammad Hadid, architect

FRUITFUL COLLABORATIONS

Minds which in lieu of exercise give themselves up to sloth; for these like the razor lose their keen edge, and the rust of ignorance destroys their form.

~ Leonardo da Vinci

Who do you admire? Who inspires you? What successful people would you like to spend time with —and why?

Leonardo kept counsel with many people he respected and admired: great mathematicians, scientists, poets, architects, alchemists, popes and kings.

One of the most fruitful collaborations of Leonardo's career occurred in 1496 when he met the mathematician Fra Luca Pacioli, during his time in Milan.

Their meeting became a catalyst for a flourishing of Leonardo's interest and development in mathematics. Leonardo was inspired by the combination of Pacioli's empirical approach with a Platonic reverence for the mystery of mathematical order.

Had he not spent time with the great mathematician Leonardo may never have been introduced to this new knowledge, and he wouldn't have been asked to illustrate Pacioli's work, *De Divina Proportione*. Leonardo's drawing of The *Vitruvian Man* is one of his most iconic creations.

The rapid development of Leonardo's anatomical studies was also attributed to his meeting with the exceptionally brilliant young anatomist Marcantonio della Torre.

Your muses don't have to be living, and you don't have to have met them personally. Leonardo was also influenced by Vitruvius, a Roman architect and engineer who died 15 years BC. Vitruvius believed in strength and beauty—ideals that Leonardo also made his own.

Resist the urge to go it alone. Two, three, four and more great minds will always be better than one.

Your Challenge

Connect with your heroes. Who can you learn most from? Look at who your muse or hero admires and follow these people too.

Reach out! Read their biography, study their path to success, connect on social-media. Get friendly and cultivate a relationship. Perhaps they'd be willing to mentor you.

Network and collaborate your way to success. Build authentic, powerful relationships with influencers, and turn those relationships into mutually beneficial partnerships.

Surround yourself with only people
who are going to lift you higher.

~ Oprah, businesswoman

RELATIONSHIP SUCCESS

Realize that everything connects to everything else.

~ Leonardo da Vinci

The health of your relationships is vital to your success. Leonardo da Vinci once said, "Marriage is like putting your hand into a bag of snakes in the hope of pulling out an eel."

Read into this what you will, but the theme is clear. Make good choices and marry well, keep your relationship in good health, or don't marry at all.

Divorce your job, your boss, your partner—anyone who is toxic to your health and happiness. Take the good with the bad, don't give up too easily, work at it and recognise that nothing is absolutely perfect.

But If you can't make things work, be it professionally or personally, be prepared to quit. Feeling like you're always getting your head bitten off, or you're surrounded by a vat of snakes will only impede your success.

Your Challenge

How healthy are your relationships?

Who is positively affecting your life?

Who, or what, do you need to divorce?

Women are always told, 'You're not going to make it, it's too difficult, you can't do that, don't enter this competition, you'll never win it.' They need confidence in themselves and people around them to help them to get on.

~ Dame Zaha Mohammad Hadid, architect

CONFLICT HAPPENS

*Nothing can be loved or hated
unless it is first understood.*

~ Leonardo da Vinci

While you need others to survive and thrive, success in work and in life is more likely when your relationships are harmonious. As much as we all like to get on, sometimes conflict is inevitable.

People may feel threatened by your success, they may deliberately try to thwart you, or they may misunderstand your motives and desires.

Your family and loved ones may resent the time you need to spend away from them. You may feel guilty for wanting more from your life.

As Leonardo said, the noblest pleasure is the joy of understanding. Seek first to understand, and then plan your conflict-handling strategy.

Your Challenge

What do others fear? How might this fear or anxiety bring 0ut the worst in them?

How might they want the best for you?

What are their agendas? How might they want the worst for you? Why might your success threaten them?

How sharp are your conflict resolution skills?

How are you unnecessarily or unknowingly creating conflict?

Learn from your experiences.

Perhaps others need to see, touch, feel, taste and smell your success before they can back you. Perhaps you do too! Succeed anyway!

I am a woman in process. I'm just trying like everybody else. I try to take every conflict, every experience, and learn from it. Life is never dull.

~ Oprah Winfrey, businesswoman

THE LITMUS TEST

Falsehood puts on a mask.
Nothing is hidden under the sun.

~ Leonardo da Vinci

I t's not easy to sever ties with people who were once close to
you. But sometimes the 'friendliest people' can be saboteurs. Use the litmus test—analyse the overall quality of your
friendships.

Are your friends, family, and other people close to you positive
or acidic and toxic. Do they elevate your self-belief and confidence or are they a dead weight?

Do they cheerlead your successes? Encourage you when you
stumble? Are they genuinely pleased to see you trying to
achieve the dreams, desires or ambitions you hold dear? Or do
they warn you of the perils of trying to fly?

Leonardo distanced himself from many people, including his family. He was always the black sheep—the illegitimate bastard. Even his father left him out of his will, and later when Leonardo's uncle made him sole heir of his estate, Leonardo's siblings fought for their share.

Instead of bemoaning his fate, or trying relentlessly to please them, he severed ties with those most toxic to him. I've had to do the same, as have many successful people.

Your time and energy is often better spent succeeding than striving to sweeten relationships that have turned sour.

Take comfort in the fact that often it's about them, not you. Resolve to speak no evil—if they are vile toward you, thank them for the lessons they are teaching you, wish them well and get on with your beautiful life.

I can't give you the formula for success, but I can failure. Try to please everyone you meet.

Your Challenge

What impact do toxic people have in your life? Do they erode your confidence? Self-esteem? Foster great self-doubt?

Who do you need to cut ties with? It doesn't always need to be physically. Although many successful people have had to move away from their family of origin to fly. Consider what and how you need to sever your connection from—emotionally, energetically, or spiritually.

Accept failure as part and parcel of life. It's not the opposite of success; it's an integral part of success.

~ Arianna Huffington, businesswoman

VALIDATE YOURSELF

He who truly knows has no occasion to shout.

~ Leonardo da Vinci

Validate and empower your relationship with yourself.
When you have healthy self-esteem you have mastered
the art of self-love.

You don't need to shout your worth from the roof-tops. You
don't need to say, 'Look at me! Look at me!' And you don't
need the validation of others to succeed.

"Many people want to please their peers, they want to please
other successful people, they want to be recognised by acad-
emia or hear everyone tell them how good they are. Forget
about it. Who cares? You are here to share your soul—not to
please others," encourages the author of *The Alchemist*, Paulo
Coehlo.

Your willingness to grow, change, take risks, and be open to all aspects of your soul, regardless of the opinions of others, is a sign of healthy self-esteem and your belief in your vision.

Criticism won't stop you in your tracks, praise won't sway you from your mission, your authentic work created with love and self-belief will magnetise customers and loyal fans to you. Infuse everything you do with your beautiful energy.

Your Challenge

How can you be your biggest fan?

What three things can you do today to validate yourself?

What three things do you need to let go of to care less about what others think?

Understand that the right to choose your own path is a sacred privilege. Use it. Dwell in possibility.

~ Oprah Winfrey, businesswoman

SOCIAL SAVVY

Words that do not satisfy the ear of the hearer
weary him or vex him.

~ Leonardo da Vinci

Leonardo was unique, different and unusual. He stood out from the crowd simply by following his curiosity and daring to challenge the norm. In doing so he attracted fans as well as rivals.

If you are original, different, or unusual in some way, your tendency to stand out from the crowd can make you a more visible target.

You may attract people who are jealous of you, and may act out angrily or violently to try and sabotage your success.

Staying strong and grounded while still keeping true to your unique vision and quest requires resilience, and the ability to develop 'social savvy.'

This is where cultivating the right mindset is important. If you think like a victim, or believe that you get scapegoated in family or other social groups you will find it difficult to get along with others and live in society.

An important diplomatic skill to master, says psychiatrist and neuroscientist Dr Mona Lisa Schulz, is assertiveness—the ability to say the right thing to the right person with the right amount of emotional intensity.

Your Challenge

How assertive are you? Do you know how to handle another person's anger, jealousy or hostility? Socially savvy people who are diplomatic either address it directly, diffuse it (humour, compassion etc.) or ignore it.

Their strategy differs depending on the situation. Whatever strategy you choose ensure that you don't become so paralysed by conflict that you become submissive, defensive, or in any way disempowered.

Critically—do not give up, or fade into obscurity. To survive in any society, or in your family tribe, master the art of knowing when to blend in, and when to be courageously different

How can you still feel good about yourself if someone is angry with you, discouraging, or jealous of your success?

A combination of good timing, flexibility, and empathy makes some people socially brilliant.

~ Dr. Mona Lisa Schulz, neuroscientist

BELONG TO YOURSELF

If you are alone you belong entirely to yourself. If you are accompanied by even one companion you belong only half to yourself or even less in proportion to the thoughtlessness of his conduct.

~ Leonardo da Vinci

You may have heard people say that you're only as successful as the five people you associate with.

As you've read, Leonardo kept counsel with many people he respected and admired. Spending time with these people no doubt fuelled his interest, inspired desire, and propelled his success.

But when it came time to do his work, he did it alone, and he did it his way. To succeed you must know when, and how, to spend time with others and when to immerse yourself in solitude.

When you do spend time with others, chose carefully. Don't dilute your energy. Too much group think can stifle your confidence, motivation and originality.

Being solitary is not the same as being a loner. Learn from others but cultivate a good relationship with yourself.

Your Challenge

Set aside some regular "you" time.

Keep your own counsel.

Love you more.

Love wins. It does win.
We know it wins.

~ J.K. Rowling, author

BALANCING RESPONSIBILITES TO OTHERS

In serving others I cannot do enough.

~ Leonardo da Vinci

Leonardo was devoid of family responsibilities—he never married and he had no children. Although he did feel responsible for housing, feeding and paying the salaries of his assistants.

If you're like me, and have family—sons or daughters at home, ageing parents, in-laws, or a spouse and partner—you'll know how hard it is to balance everybody's needs. So many people, women in particular, feel guilty putting their needs first.

But somewhere you have to take time for you! If you aways give, give to others, there'll come point when the well is dry. At some point you have to prioritise your needs, dreams and ambitions—and your sanity. Leonardo knew this too. No matter how much you have on your dinner plate you can make room for you.

Your Challenge

Are mistaken beliefs about pursuing your own desires holding you back?

Are you being a martyr? Doing everything for everyone? Or do you delegate and enlist others to help?

The moment you are old enough to take the wheel, responsibility lies with you.

~ J.K. Rowling, author

STAY AHEAD OF THE COMPETITION

What is fair in men, passes away, but not so in art.

~ Leonardo da Vinci

You must know what others are doing in order to perform better. Learn from your competitors.

Work-wise you are in competition for the discretionary income of current and future customers, just as Leonardo was. He constantly innovated to stay ahead of his rivals. But he drew ideas from them too.

Relationship-wise you may be in competition with people who want what you've got.

Knowing your competition should not be something that stresses you out. Understanding what others are doing right, or different from you can inspire.

You'll know when to lift your game and when to shape-shift

and start anew. When too many like-minded talents flood the market, you may 'do a Leonardo'—diversify, adapt and move.

Michelangelo, Raphael, Botticelli and other artists all competed with Leonardo for sought after commissions that only a few wealthy patrons could provide.

During his later years in Milan, Leonardo fell out of favour with the Medici pope. But once again he turned his misfortunate into fortune, aligning with the French king and moving to France where his competitors would be few. There he created some of his best art and began at last to compile his lifetime's work into his treatise.

Your Challenge

Here's a few ways to stay ahead of the competition:

- Keep your eyes on your rivals
- Know your stakeholders and treat them well
- Differentiate yourself from your competitors
- Step up your marketing
- Target new markets
- Diversify and expand your offer
- Look to the future
- Innovate—be a pioneer
- Keeping improving—good art endures.

Life is an unfoldment, and the further we travel the more truth we can comprehend. To understand the things that are at our door is the best preparation for understanding those that lie beyond.

~ Hypatia of Alexandria, astronomer

PRINCIPLE SEVEN: EMPOWER YOUR WORK

BE ORIGINAL

The painter will produce pictures of little merit if he takes the works of others as his standard.

~ Leonardo da Vinci

Originality and authenticity was a crucial part of Leonardo's success. HIs obsessive search for original truth, understanding and invention led him to create things other thought were crazy or impossible—but later copied or followed.

A big part of authenticity is following your own truth. If you think something is a great idea—try it. Don't get bogged down subscribing to other people's ideas and taking their work as your standard.

Be a trailblazer like all the great inventors, and have the satisfaction of being authentically you.

History is richer because of people, like Leonardo da Vinci, who strode forward despite others rejecting their attempts, laughing at their vision, or criticising them personally and professionally. Original thinkers, feelers and believers always see things others don't.

Your Challenge

Determine who you are and who you choose to be.

Create a life or work of heart that is as original as you are. Believe in your capacity for originality.

Take your opinion as your standard. Bring forth your passion and infuse your life and work with true essence—all else will follow.

I had no idea that being your authentic self could make me as rich as I've become. If I had, I'd have done it a lot earlier.

~ Oprah Winfrey, businesswoman

LIST YOUR THINGS TO DO

It is useful to constantly observe, note, and consider.

~ Leonardo da Vinci

L eonardo used to travel with a small notebook hanging from his belt so that whenever something caught his eye he could make a note, or record it visually. His genius lay in knowing that not everything that could be recorded and stored in the mind.

His mind was restlessly hungry. There were so many things he wanted to do. So that no opportunity was left untapped his notebooks and journals served as his 'to do' list.

Here's a few things translated from the tumble of thoughts recorded in his journals:

- Draw Milan
- Find a master of hydraulics and get him to tell you how to repair a lock, canal and mill

- Ask about the measurement of the sun

Leonardo, like other great brains, allowed his mind to free-range. No single idea could hold his interest indefinitely. The task and challenge of marshalling his thoughts into a coherent, structured whole fell to others.

Forcing yourself to concentrate prematurely can inhibit your imagination. Far better, Leonardo and other creativity experts maintain, to record inspiration as it strikes, in a to-do-some-time-in the-future list.

Studies, including one by Dr. Holly White, then at the University of Memphis, found that minds that break-free, that naturally wander, can often achieve more than those which are more ordered, structured—and arguably, inhibited.

Your Challenge

Where do you record your great ideas? Small seeds of inspiration can blossom into formidable majesty.

Sustain you focus and future potential by down jotting thoughts, as and when they occur, for future reference.

I found I could say things with colour
and shapes that I couldn't say any other way—things I had no
words for.

~ Georgia O'Keeffe, artist

MAKE YOUR JOB WORK FOR YOU

As you cannot do what you want,
Want what you can do.

~ Leonardo da Vinci

Leonardo cultivated successful relationships and actively sought wealthy benefactors to finance his ambitions. He worked for tyrants, murderers and fools when he needed to finance his passions.

While he loved his freedom he was also a pragmatist. Court appointments were in many ways an ideal position for Leonardo. They took away the pressure of depending upon erratic commissions which independent artists relied on.

By taking away money worries, and coming under the protection of powerful rulers, it gave him time to explore all of his passions and interests while earning a steady salary.

On the flip-side though, much of this time was consumed

fulfilling his employers' desires. Sometimes these bosses, like Cesare Borgia, were tyrannical murderers— conflicting with Leonardo's values.

Leonardo knew that maintaining a positive attitude was critical, as was making sure his passion projects weren't neglected.

"Evil thinking is either envy or ingratitude", he once wrote. He was grateful for those who paid his bills, but the pursuit of gold was never his primary driver.

If you can't have what you want, learn to love what you've got. Attitude is queen.

Your Challenge

If you feel trapped or stifled by your current job or boss, how can you maintain a positive mindset?

How can you finance your passions?

Do you need to make peace with those who pay your bills?

Don't be afraid to take time to learn. It's good to work for other people. I worked for others for 20 years. They paid me to learn.

~ Vera Wang, designer

THE MONEY OR YOUR LIFE

It may be that I shall possess less than other men of more peaceful lives, or than those who want to grow rich in a day. I may live for a long time in great poverty, as always happens, and to all eternity will happen, to alchemists, the would-be creators of gold and silver.

~ Leonardo da Vinci

Money gives you choices, but the pursuit of wealth is not everything. Like Leonardo, having mountains of gold and silver may not be your primary motivator.

Throughout this book I've encouraged you to work out what is really true for you. Prioritising the value you place on money, amassing a fortune and material wealth may create a massive mindset shift.

Your Challenge

What are the hidden costs of always striving for money?

What can you start, stop, do more, less of to earn less but live more?

IF LACK of finances are a challenge for you you'll find plenty of creative and practical ways to do more with less, or generate more cash-flow in my *Mid-Life Career Rescue* trilogy.

> *You only have what you give.*
> *It's by spending yourself that you become rich.*

> ~ Isabel Allende, author

STEAL LIKE AN ARTIST

He is a poor pupil who does not go beyond his master.

~ Leonardo da Vinci

A foundation step to fast-track success is to follow the things you love and learn from those who have made this love a key part of their success.

"School is one thing. Education is another,"writes Austin Kleon in, *Steal Like an Artist*. Acquire knowledge as Leonardo did. Learn your way to success.

Leonardo started his career as a child copying and drawing nature. His inspiration drove his quest. He followed his curiosity and the things he loved.

Early in his career he was apprenticed to Andrea del Verrocchio, from whom Leonardo copied how to make brushes, prepare paint, draw, sculpt and paint.

The story of Leonardo surpassing his master is legendary—the angel he added to Verrocchio's painting (*Baptism of Christ*, c. 1473) was so much better that the master never painted again.

At the young age of 21 Leonardo designed and completed a painting on his own, *The Annunciation*. Just think how much slower his progress would have been had he not studied under a master.

You may not have access to a mentor or teacher physically, but you can align mentally, emotionally, and spiritually.

Your Challenge

Read biographies, study the work of those whose success you'd love to emulate. Think about your favourite heros and heroines —in business and in life. Google everything!

Copycat your way to success and then take it a step further. What did they miss? What could have been better? What didn't they do? If all your favourite muses got together what would they be making today?

Then go make that stuff.

I do not try to dance better than anyone else. I only try to dance better than myself.

~ Arianna Huffington, businesswoman

STEP BY STEP

If you wish to go to the top of a building, you must go up step by step; otherwise it will be impossible that you should reach the top.

~ Leonardo da Vinci

So many people rush in the climb for success, ignoring planning and tripping over their lack of knowledge, and the practical skills that must be learned. Anyone can be good but being exceptional takes diligence.

Leonardo da Vinci said that if you wish to pursue your craft, and have a sound knowledge of a subject, you need to identify the details you need to master.

Begin at the first step, "And do not go onto the second step till you have the first well fixed in memory and in practice. And if you do otherwise you will throw away your time, or certainly greatly prolong your studies. And remember to acquire diligence rather than rapidity."

Avoid being controlled and dictated to by the relentless ticking clock. Little steps are more effective than grand leaps so don't become disheartened or be deterred if your progress is slower than others. Do something every day, no matter how small, to keep your dreams alive.

Your Challenge

What does being diligent mean to you?

Have you identified all the knowledge and skills and steps you need to master in order to achieve your successful outcome?

Are you patient or impatient? How could rushing to the outcome trip you up?

Today we often use deadlines, real and imaginary,
to imprison ourselves.

~ Arianna Huffington, businesswoman

DO WHAT YOU ARE

The acquisition of knowledge is always of use to the intellect,
because it may thus drive out useless things and retain the good.

~ Leonardo da Vinci

While Leonardo clearly didn't have access to modern personality tests, he was a master in the realms of observation. He knew what gave him energy, how he preferred to take in information, make decisions and organise his life.

The Myers-Briggs Type Indicator is one of the most popular preference-based tools. Experts differ in whether Leonardo's personality preferences were INTP (Introverted, Intuitive, Thinking, and Perceiving), or ISTP (Introverted, Sensing, Thinking, and Perceiving), or even an ENTP (Extroverted, Intuitive, Thinking, and Perceiving.

I know some of these terms may be foreign to you. See the Further Resources section at the end of this book for more information about The Myers-Briggs Type Indicator, or turn to Google.

While guessing people preferences accurately is not possible, my bet is Leonardo's leaned toward INTP. His thinking was highly introverted and intuitive as evidenced by his prolific recording of thoughts and ideas recorded in his extensive collection of journals.

His thoughts were diverted into many areas of interest and many of his works remain uncompleted—something that would drive a Judging type crazy. And he preferred the company of special friends and colleagues rather than the mass gatherings and membership of large groups.

Also he was an outlier in so many areas.

Research suggests that less than 10 percent of the population are (INTPs) Introverted, Intuitive, Thinking, and Perceivers— putting Leonardo once again at odds with mainstream folk. More so in Italy, which as a country shares a reported domi- nant preference for ENFP.

Neuropsychologist, Katherine Benziger says, "People are happi- est, healthiest and most effective when developing, using and being rewarded for using their natural gifts." This is very true.

The more you know about yourself the happier you'll be. The better your decisions will be and the more chance you will have of presenting yourself and your natural talents in the best light to people—including yourself.

Your Challenge

What are your natural gifts? What are your super powers?

How can you do and be what you are?

See the Further Resources section at the end of this book for more information about The Myers Briggs Type Indicator.

Find something that you love to do, and find a place that you really like to do it in. Your work has to be compelling. You spend a lot of time doing it.

~ Ursula Burns, CEO

KNOW WHEN TO QUIT

Art is never finished, only abandoned.

~ Leonardo da Vinci

Leonardo was criticised for the number of times he left work unfinished. But given his personality preferences and motivations, the chances are high he got bored.

Leonardo thrived on solving challenging problems, starting and visualising new work, more than he did in the operational tasks required for completion.

He also liked to be his own master, and create work in line with his far-reaching and unconventional vision.

Back in the 15th century the role of an artist during the Renaissance was only just beginning to change from mere tool-boy, to master artisan and rockstar.

Many of Leonardo's patrons had control over the subject

matter of what he painted, and how he was to paint it—including the minerals and colours.

These, and the many other constraints exerted upon a creative thinker, free-spirit and highly intelligent man like Leonardo, killed his joy.

Records show he was not always paid for his work, and often struggled financially. Whatever the reasons for his disinterest in continuing with projects, Leonardo knew when to quit.

He was also a strategic player, seldom did he move on without something else to occupy himself. Abandoning displeasing, late-paying clients for more lucrative practical realities was a smart move. As was diversifying and setting the bar higher.

Refusing to settle for mediocrity sustained him—as it will you.

Your Challenge

If you're bored, if you don't feel a shiver of excitement or fear, if there's no emotional risk involved, let it go…abandon ship.

If you're struggling to pay the bills, know when to persevere or when it's best to quit You can always return, as Leonardo did, when the timing is better.

You are the storyteller of your own life, and you can create your own legend, or not.

~ Isabel Allende, author

GET OUT OF YOUR OWN WAY

Fortune is powerless to help one
who does not exert himself.

~ Leonardo da Vinci

So many people who took The Art of Success Questionnaire asked me, "How do I get out of my own way?" Inspiration has to find you working. It won't come any faster or slower with excuses, tricks, 'pretend' deadlines, or bribes.

As Paulo Coelho, author of *The Alchemist*, said on *The Tim Ferris Show* recently, "I have the book inside me, I start procrastinating in the morning. I check my emails, I check news—I check anything that I could check just to avoid the moment to sit and face myself as a writer in front of my book.

For three hours I am trying to tell myself, 'No, no, no. Later. Later. Later.' Then later not to lose face in front of myself I tell myself to sit and write for half an hour, and of course this half an hour becomes 10 hours in a row. That's why I write my books so quickly. Very quickly, because I cannot stop. I cannot stop."

Your Challenge

Hack through your excuses: "You're too tired. You don't have time. You're not feeling inspired. It's not good enough. It's not perfect." Or whatever stories you tell yourself to avoid working.

Your excuses are your saboteurs. Your doubts—your traitors. Just do the work. But do it well and do it to the best of your abilities. It's amazing how much can be achieved when you stop resisting.

Identify how you get in your own way. Be honest.

Make a commitment to overcome your SELF.

Make a commitment to really follow your dream.

Do the work! Set a time-limit if it helps. Just 30 minutes—then watch as you get carried away.

The days you work are the best days.

~ Georgia O'Keeffe, artist

PATIENT PERSERVERANCE

Patience preserves us against insults precisely as clothes do against the cold. For if you multiply your garment as the cold increases, that cold cannot hurt you; in the same way increase your patience under great offences, and they cannot hurt your feelings.

~ Leonardo da Vinci

Knowing when to quit is one thing; knowing when to persevere another. Whether it's the weight of obstacles you face, the setbacks and the disappointments, the successes others seem to more speedily achieve, or the critical feedback from others impatient to see more evidence you'll make it— never give up.

Never, never, never give up.

Many of Leonardo's greatest and most enduring successes took years and years to achieve. For over four years he persevered with painting The Mona Lisa. And while modern critics claim he never finished it, it doesn't seem to have mattered in the end.

It wasn't good enough. It was better.

Through his patience, persistence and perseverance he, and his artworks, have achieved immortality.

Your Challenge

Keep your mind on your vision, your body moving towards your dreams, your heart warmed by the joy you will feel when you finally achieve success. Most of all enjoy whatever you choose to be, have or do.

Every day see and feel your dream as though it is already achieved, hear the feedback you will receive, taste the victory of your success.

This will keep your faith alive, empower your dreams with your energy, fortify your tenacity—attracting what and who you need, when you need it.

If self-doubt increases, confidence wanes or some other saboteur infects your psyche, dig into your toolkit and multiply your armour. Fortify yourself. Increase your patience—persist and persevere. Success could be just around the corner.

When you think of patience, perseverance and success who comes to mind?

Who or what can help you manifest more persistence?

Identify three ways to strengthen your persistence by strengthening your willpower and self-discipline.

He who wishes to be rich within a day,
will be hanged within a year.

~ Leonardo da Vinci, inventor

PURSUE YOUR TRUTH

Fire destroys all sophistry, that is, deceit;
and maintains truth alone, that is gold.
Truth at last cannot be hidden.

~ Leonardo da Vinci

Truth is where the magic is. "Truth—the sun. Falsehood —a mask", Leonardo once wrote in his journal. Take off your mask, forget about pleasing others. Please yourself. The pursuit of truth is not always comfortable as many of the great trail-blazers can testify.

All the successful men and women I admire, Leonardo da Vinci included, have searched for and followed their truth— and fought for it. They would rather be failures at something they believed in, then amass success built on a brittle pyre of lies.

Success doesn't come in a manual with fail-safe instructions and money-back guarantees. But there is one truth no one can deny—when you work with integrity and imbue your efforts with love you draw others to you.

As I've already mentioned, love is the highest, most powerful vibration on earth. When you work with love people feel it. It infuses everything you do and attracts people who are magnetised by this potent energy to you. That's why love, truth and beauty are the best marketing tools around.

Here's a few things following your truth may do for you:

- Liberate you
- Liberate others
- Empower your success
- Lead you to discover new realities
- Energise you
- Attract like-minded people to you
- Boost your courage, confidence and self-belief
- Fill your soul with fire and your heart with passion.

Your Challenge

If you wish to succeed in business and life there are two questions you must ask: who are you and are you following your truth?

Choose to fulfil your potential and make something of your life. I believe in you. Go create joy, beauty, love, and magic!

The best way to change it is to do it. Right? And then after a while you become it, and it's easy.

~ Ursula Burns, CEO

COLOUR YOUR SUCCESS

Among the various studies of natural processes,
that of light gives most pleasure to those who contemplate it.

~ Leonardo da Vinci

The magical power of colour to transform, uplift and empower is something Leonardo was intimately acquainted with.

Psychologists, marketers and brand gurus all know that surrounding yourself with the right colours can mean the difference between failure and success.

Research reveals that it only takes 90 seconds to assess and make a subconscious visual judgement, and a massive 62 to 90 percent of that judgement is based on colour alone.

People's beliefs about the power of colour to boost their success include:

- 92 percent believe colour presents an image of impressive quality
- 90 percent feel colour can assist in attracting new customers
- 90 percent believe customers remember presentations and documents better when colour is used
- 83 percent believe colour makes them appear more successful
- 81 percent think colour gives them a competitive edge
- 76 percent believe that the use of colour makes their business appear larger to clients

And let's not forget how surrounding yourself with colour makes you feel. Add to this the potent power of naturally occurring minerals, gems and metamorphic rocks mined from the earth, and you have potent alchemy.

Mona Lisa continues to be one of the world's most memorable and enchanting portraits. It's no coincidence that Leonardo painted the mesmerising bright blue sky surrounding her with Lapis lazuli. Sadly, time has diluted the original colour but the magic remains.

Lapis Lazuli (a bright blue metamorphic rock consisting largely of lazurite) is known as the 'visionary's stone.' It is associated with wisdom and spiritual insight, the promotion of truth, and is also believed to strengthen the mind, enhance psychic abilities, and enable a higher connection with your Higher Self and Spirit Guides.

These are principles and abilities that Leonardo valued highly. It's no coincidence that he painted the powerful blue sky surrounding the Mona Lisa with Lapis lazuli. Mona Lisa continues to be one of world's most enchanting portraits.

Colours have such an impact on your emotions and actions that it makes sense to wear your success colours. Leonardo loved purples—colours associated with nobility as well as the ability to access higher levels of spirituality.

Me? I love gold. Gold makes me feel enriched, nourished, blessed, strong. I used to live in a gold house, and when I need a boost of morale I put on my gold dress! Whatever works, right?!

Your Challenge

What is your success colour?

How could you surround yourself with more of this colour to fuel your success?

The best colour in the whole world,
is the one that looks good, on you!

~ Coco Chanel, fashion designer

YOUR BEAUTY SPOT

What induces you, oh man, to depart from your home in town, to leave parents and friends, and go to the countryside over mountains and valleys, if it is not for the beauty of the world of nature.

~ Leonardo da Vinci

Your Beauty Spot Is Your Point of Brilliance

If you've read my other books you'll know that I've always loved what the artist and philosopher John Ruskin once said, "Where talent, interest and motivation intersect expect a masterpiece."

Using this as your guide, you may like to draw three circles. List your areas of motivation in one (passion, purpose, values, goals etc.); Your interests and obsessions in another; Your favourite skills and talents in the third.

Note where they overlap. This is your internal world, and what

I have in the past called your PassionPoint, or Point of Brilliance.

It's also your beauty spot. It's where love lives. It's the union of your soul—your path with heart which leads you toward your higher purpose. As Leonardo said, without love, what then? It's where your light shines brightest.

Surround these three circles with a fourth to enclose them. This symbolises the external world—both the practical earth and the higher heavens. So many people have speculated on and sensationalised Leonardo's greatest works, looking for clues to interpret and break codes to discover sacred mysteries.

But as Leonardo said himself, the truth is best left in the open. That which is above is the same as that which is below. And this is where beauty and success unite.

Leonardo remains an enigma. But we do know he communed with the Universe, saw into the future, and worked damned hard to master his talents and bring his visions into living realities.

How Can Your Point Of Brilliance Serve?

To generate career options, knowing what will be needed or in demand, now and in the future, can yield gold.

What needs can you fulfil when you're aligned with your beauty spot? What economic, demographic, social, environmental or other needs can you serve? This is the work you are called to do and where you will truly shine.

It doesn't need to have a massive job title, or be about saving the world. But whatever you choose to do has to fulfil a need. Economics 101—no need, no demand.

Of course, if money is no barrier, you are freer to pursue your own needs without this added focus. By doing this you may just create a demand, or make the world a happier place. Importantly, you'll be happy.

Remember Your Criteria for Success

So many people embark on one path only to find it cuts or suffocates other choices. Others mistakenly believe that you can't have a multitude of passions.

Be clear about who you are, what success means to you, your criteria for fulfilment and begin with this end in mind. Work backwards from the future to implement your success strategy.

CONCLUSION

CONCLUSION: BEAUTY AND THE BEST

"The heavens often rained down the richest gifts on human beings, naturally, but sometimes with lavish abundance bestow upon a single individual beauty, grace and ability, so that, whatever he does, every action is so divine that he distances all other men, and clearly displays how his genius is the gift of God and not a requirement of human art."

~ Giorgio Vasari, *Lives of The Artists*

The belief in the creative, regenerative and divine (transcendental) power of beauty was central to everything Leonardo da Vinci pursued.

Inspired by Vitruvius and the architecture of success grounded in the ancient wisdom of Pythagorean and Platonic mathematical principals, Leonardo knew that nature held the immortal secrets of both beauty and power.

While Leonardo is arguably most famous as an artist, he was the archetype of a Renaissance man, whose unquenchable curiosity was equalled only by the power of his imagination and aptitude for invention.

He gave birth to knowledge that some 500 years later is enjoying its own renaissance, and is validated by modern science (itself only a relatively young 300 years old).

Beauty is timeless, holding sacred universal wisdom and truth. The artist Paul Klee once said, 'One eye sees and the other feels'. And it is this ability to make us care where Leonardo has surpassed many others.

Beauty And Your Success

Beauty comes from the inside. It's your essence—so authentic that, just as there will never be another Leonardo, there will never be another you.

The art of success lies in bringing more beauty into this world. It lies in being you. It's a secret that ancient masters and philosophers understood well. And it's a secret that modern day successful people also know and harness.

Businessmen and women, politicians, and the most successful artists understand that intrinsic, authentic, soulful beauty attracts. Beauty is irresistible. Beauty sells.

You may not be aiming to create the next *Mona Lisa*, but if you infuse your life and your work with your energy, power, talent and essence, who knows—500 years from today somebody may well be writing a book about you and the legacy you left.

You may think the outcome has to happen in a certain way, on a certain day, to reach your goal. But human willpower cannot make everything happen. Spirit has its own idea, of how the arrow flies, and upon what wind it travels.

It may not happen overnight, but if you maintain your focus, and take inspired action, and follow your heart, your time will come.

I promise!

If due to some strange twist of fate, it doesn't? At least you'll know you tried.

A life of no regrets—now that's worth striving for.

Let the beauty you love be the life that you live. Now go out and create great art!

IN GRATITUDE AND WITH LOVE,

Cassandra

THE TRUTH ABOUT SUCCESS

The love of virtue. It never looks at any vile or base thing, but rather clings always to pure and virtuous things and takes up its abode in a noble heart;
as the birds do in green woods on flowery branches. And this Love shows itself more in adversity than in prosperity; as light does, which shines most where the place is darkest.

~ Leonardo da Vinci

I've distilled Leonardo's principles for success down to twenty-one facts...or TRUTHS as I call them. And the wonderful thing is that these truths can be embodied by you. You can be, have and do whatever your heart desires if you're determined to succeed and look for ways to put these truths into practice.

\# 1 Love

\# 2 Talent

#3 Curiosity

#4 Learning

#5 Interest

#6 Vision

7 Service/Purpose

8 Opportunity

#9 Focus

#10 Commitment

#11 Values

#12 Motivation

#13 Labour

#14 Asking

#15 Goals

#16 Optimism

#17 Virtue/Integrity

#I18 Instinct

#19 Gratitude

#20 Energy

#21 Play

I KNOW you can succeed at whatever you set your heart, mind and soul to. Pursue your liberty—be free to be you.

Have the courage and confidence to define success on your own terms.

Follow your passions, cultivate your natural and dormant talents, remain curious and embrace learning, follow your interests, maintain your vision, work with purpose and be of service.

When opportunity knocks, open the door. If it doesn't knock, go out and create opportunities. Focus on what you desire, not what you fear. Commit—devote yourself to your quest for success.

Let your values guide you—they are your truth-compass. Clarify what motivates you, be this extrinsic or intrinsic rewards. Do the work—no matter how small the effort, in time you will amass success.

Ask your way to success, and learn from those with the skill, knowledge and power to help you. Don't be shy, proud or nervous to ask for help!

Set goals—little, bigger and bigger still. Stretch and grow and strive to make the impossible possible. Celebrate your successes along the way—no matter how small.

Cultivate optimism—water it regular and never let faith and hope wither from neglect.

Maintain your integrity and virtue. Follow your hunches, intuition and instinct. Be grateful for all that you have—be it health, friends, support, or your cat.

Maximise your energy—look after your mind, body and soul. And lastly, but perhaps also firstly, play.

Alleviate the pressure—don't take yourself too seriously. Be joyful in success—and also while attempting success. Keep your feet on the ground, your head in the clouds and ride the magic carpet of your creative imagination.

But most of all, 'do a Leonardo'—stand out from the crowd and dare to be different!

Secretly we're all a little more absurd
than we make ourselves out to be.

~ J.K. Rowling, author

If the painter wishes to see beauties that charm him, it lies in his power to create them, and if he wishes to see monstrosities that are frightful, ridiculous, or truly pitiable, he is lord and God thereof.

~ Leonardo da Vinci, 1472

PLEASE LEAVE A REVIEW

Word of mouth is the most powerful marketing force in the universe. If you found this book useful, I'd appreciate you rating this book and leaving a review. You don't have to say much—just a few words about how the book helped you learn something new or made you feel.

"Your books are a fantastic resource and until now I never even thought to write a review. Going forward I will be reviewing more books. So many great ones out there and I want to support the amazing people that write them."

Great reviews help people find good books.

Thank you so much! I appreciate you!

PS: If you enjoyed this book, do me a small favour to help spread the word about it and share on Facebook, Twitter and other social networks.

ABOUT THE AUTHOR

Cassandra Gaisford, is a holistic therapist, award-winning artist, and #1 bestselling author. A corporate escapee, she now lives and works from her idyllic lifestyle property overlooking the Bay of Islands in New Zealand.

Cassandra is best known for the passionate call to redefine what it means to be successful in today's world.

She is a well-known expert in the area of success, passion, purpose and transformational business, career and life change, and is regularly sought after as a keynote speaker, and by media seeking an expert opinion on career and personal development issues.

Cassandra has also contributed to international publications and been interviewed on national radio and television in New Zealand and America.

She has a proven-track record of success helping people find savvy ways to boost their finances, change careers, build a business or become a solopreneur—on a shoestring.

Cassandra's unique blend of business experience and qualifications (BCA, Dip Psych.), creative skills, and well-ness and holistic training (Dip Counselling, Reiki Master Teacher) blends pragmatism and commercial savvy with rare and unique insight and out-of-the-box-thinking for anyone wanting to achieve an extraordinary life.

ALSO BY CASSANDRA GAISFORD

Transformational Super Kids:

The Little Princess
The Little Princess Can Fly
I Have to Grow
The Boy Who Cried
Jojo Lost Her Confidence

Mid-Life Career Rescue:

The Call for Change
What Makes You Happy
Employ Yourself
Job Search Strategies That Work
3 Book Box Set: The Call for Change, What Makes You Happy,
Employ Yourself
4 Book Box Set: The Call for Change, What Makes You Happy,
Employ Yourself, Job Search Strategies That Work

Career Change:

Career Change 2020 5 Book-Bundle Box Set

Master Life Coach:

Leonardo da Vinci: Life Coach
Coco Chanel: Life Coach

The Art of Living:

How to Find Your Passion and Purpose
How to Find Your Passion and Purpose Companion Workbook
Career Rescue: The Art and Science of Reinventing Your Career and Life
Boost Your Self-Esteem and Confidence
Anxiety Rescue
No! Why 'No' is the New 'Yes'
How to Find Your Joy and Purpose
How to Find Your Joy and Purpose Companion Workbook

The Art of Success:

Leonardo da Vinci
Coco Chanel

Journaling Prompts Series:

The Passion Journal
The Passion-Driven Business Planning Journal
How to Find Your Passion and Purpose 2 Book-Bundle Box Set

Health & Happiness:

The Happy, Healthy Artist
Stress Less. Love Life More
Bounce: Overcoming Adversity, Building Resilience and
Finding Joy
Bounce Companion Workbook

Mindful Sobriety:

Mind Your Drink: The Surprising Joy of Sobriety
Mind Over Mojitos: How Moderating Your Drinking Can
Change Your Life: Easy Recipes for Happier Hours & a
Joy-Filled Life
Your Beautiful Brain: Control Alcohol and Love Life More

Happy Sobriety:

Happy Sobriety: Non-Alcoholic Guilt-Free Drinks You'll Love
The Sobriety Journal
Happy Sobriety Two Book Bundle-Box Set: Alcohol and Guilt-Free
Drinks You'll Love & *The Sobriety Journal*

Money Manifestation:

Financial Rescue: The Total Money Makeover: Create Wealth,
Reduce Debt & Gain Freedom

The Prosperous Author:

Developing a Millionaire Mindset
Productivity Hacks: Do Less & Make More
Two Book Bundle-Box Set (Books 1-2)

Miracle Mindset:

Change Your Mindset: Millionaire Mindset Makeover: The Power of Purpose, Passion, & Perseverance

Non-Fiction:

Where is Salvator Mundi?

More of Cassandra's practical and inspiring workbooks on a range of career and life-enhancing topics are on her website (www.cassandragaisford.com) and her author page at all good online bookstores.

COACHING AND WELLNESS THERAPIES

If you could free yourself from everything holding you back from living an incredible life —all of your fears, stinkin' thinking, limiting beliefs, negative emotions —you know you'd instantly feel happier, healthier and freer, right? But how? How can you liberate yourself from all that obstacles and blocks preventing you from living your best life?

The solution is so simple. Whether you have lost your job or hate the one you have, your relationship has hit a rough patch, or you're struggling with anxiety, depression, addiction or any other issues are impacting your life, talking to an impartial professional, qualified holistic therapist, counsellor, and life coach can help.

I offer a range of transformational life and career rescue remedies, including:

• **Quantum Transformational Coaching** *(QTC)* to rapidly breakthrough limiting beliefs, sabotaging thoughts, subconscious blocks, and outdated scripts that are holding you back.

• **Akashic Records Soul Reading**—Unlock your destiny, heal the past, manifest a wonderful future. Achieve truly transformational and life-changing results fast.

• **Career Counselling** to help resolve career-related issues such as stress, role-conflict, job loss, workplace bullying, dissatisfaction, and assistance with career reinvention planning and self-employment coaching,

• **Personal therapy** provides early, solutions-focused intervention before problems escalate. A holistic approach to resolving many non-work issues including relationships, finances, physical and emotional well-being stress, grief, conflict, depression, lack of self-esteem, substance abuse...and more.

• **Life coaching** to help you when you don't need in-depth counselling. You may just be feeling stuck, lost, or demotivated, and need someone objective and supportive (and sometimes bossy!) to spur you on. Life coaching is solutions-focused, and rather than dwell on the past, focuses on where you are now, where you want to be and the steps and changes necessary to get you there

Live and work with purpose, passion, and prosperity no matter where you are in New Zealand or the world. I can help you reach your potential by phone, Skype or by e-mail. Schedule an appointment here—I'd love to provide guidance and support to help you live your best life.

Or, navigate to the following page to learn more about my wellness therapies and coaching services and how they can help you:

http://www.cassandragaisford.com/wellness-therapies/

"Thank YOU! Our coaching was immensely helpful, and I have renewed hope for finding my way. You are simply lovely, and brilliant, and wise. So glad our energies aligned, and I found you! I am also so enjoying your books and will give more feedback as I go as well as post reviews online. And they will be GLOWING, I can assure you!"

~ Lisa Webb, artist

"A coaching session with Cassandra is like a light switch to a light bulb. My ideas were there but without that light switch I wasn't able to see them and manifest my dream of running a holistic business from home. Straight away, Cassandra was able to get to the heart of my core values and how to put them into a dream business. I now have the sense of purpose and drive to achieve my business goals. Cassandra's warm personality and positive approach make her a joy to work with. I recommend her to anyone who wants to unlock their personal and professional potential."

~ Shelley Sweeney, writer & Reiki practitioner

(Did you know that coaching fees are often tax deductible for people who use coaching to improve their professional skills? Check with your accountant for details.)

FOLLOW YOUR PASSION TO PROSPERITY ONLINE COURSE

If you need more help to find and live your life purpose you may prefer to take my online course, and watch inspirational and practical videos and other strategies to help you to fulfil your potential.

Follow your passion and purpose to prosperity—online coaching program

Easily discover your passion and purpose, overcoming barriers to success, and create a job or business you love with my self-paced online course.

Gain unlimited lifetime access to this course, for as long as you like—across any and all devices you own. Be supported with practical, inspirational, easy-to-access strategies to achieve your dreams.

To start achieving outstanding personal and professional results with absolute certainty and excitement. **Click here to enrol or find out more—the-coaching-lab.teachable.com/p/follow-your-passion-and-purpose-to-prosperity**

FURTHER RESOURCES

Surf The Net

Mathew Johnstone has a wide range of books and resources on mental wellness and mindfulness: www.matthewjohnstone. com.au

www.whatthebleep.com—a powerful and inspiring site emphasizing quantum physics and the transformational power of thought.

www.heartmath.org—comprehensive information and tools help you access your intuitive insight and heart-based knowledge. Validated and supported by science-based research. Check out the additional information about your heart-brain.

Join polymath Tim Ferris and learn from his interesting and informative guests on The Tim Ferris Show http:// fourhourworkweek.com/podcast/.

Listen to podcasts which inspire you to become the best version of your writing self—*Joanna Penn's podcast* is very helpful for "authorpreneurs" http://www.thecreativepenn.com/podcasts. I also love Neil Patel's podcast for savvy marketing strategies http://neilpatel.com/podcast.

Experience the transformative power of hypnosis. One of my favorite hypnosis sites is the UK-based Uncommon Knowledge. On their website http://www.hypnosisdownloads.com you'll find a range of self-hypnosis mp3 audios, including The Millionaire Mindset program.

Celebrity hypnotherapist and author Marissa Peer is another favorite source of subconscious reprogramming and liberation —www.marisapeer.com.

What beliefs are holding you back? Check out Peer's Youtube clip "How To Teach Your Mind That Everything Is Available To You" here—https://www.youtube.com/watch?v=IKeaAbM2kJg

Enjoy James Clear's fabulous blog content and receive further self-improvement tips based on proven scientific research: http://jamesclear.com/articles

Tim Ferriss recommends a couple of apps for those wanting some help getting started with meditation—Headspace (www.headspace.com) or Calm (www.calm.com).

National Geographic: The Science of Stress: Portrait of a killer

https://www.youtube.com/watch?v=ZyBsy5SQxqU

Effects of Stress on Your Body

https://www.youtube.com/watch?v=1p6EeYwp1O4

Mindfulness training

Wellington-based Peter Fernando offers an introductory guided meditation which you can take further. He also meets with individuals and groups in Wellington for philosophical talks on mindfulness and Buddhism. Very enjoyable and great for the soul.

http://www.monthofmindfulness.info

Guided meditations

www.calm.com

Free app with guided meditations

http://eocinstitute.org/meditation/emotional-benefits-of-meditation/

Includes a comprehensive list of the benefits of meditation.

Career Guidance Sites:

www.aarp.org/work - information and tools to help you stay current and connected with what's hot and what's not in today's workplace.

www.lifereimagined.org - loads of inspiration and practical

tips to help you maximise your interests and expertise, personalised and interactive.

www.whatthebleep.com – a powerful and inspiring site emphasising quantum physics and the transformational power of thought.

www.personalitytype.com—created by the authors of *Do What You Are: Discover the Perfect Career for You through the Secrets of Personality Type*. This site focuses on expanding your awareness of your own type and that of others—including children and partners. This site also contains many useful links.

Books

Spirituality meets science in Deepak Chopra's transformational book, *How to Know God: The Soul's Journey into the Mystery of Mysteries*

Laura Charanza shares her story in *Ugly Love: A Survivor's Story of Narcissistic Abuse.*

When Pleasing You Is Killing Me, Dr. Les Carter takes you inside his counselling office, inviting you to share in real life stories of people just like you who are trying to make sense of persistent, controlling demands from all sorts of controlling people.

A Technique for Meditation, by Joseph Polansky explores spiritual cause and remedies for modern dis-ease, including the importance of being in harmony with your Higher Genuis.

Master your millionaire mindset with T. Harv Eker's book,

Secrets of the Millionaire Mind: Mastering the Inner Game of Wealth.

Find your ONE thing with Gary Keller in *The One Thing: The Surprisingly Simple Truth Behind Extraordinary Results.*

Learn from masters in a diverse cross-section of fields—pick up a copy of Tim Ferriss' *Tool of Titans.*

Celebrate being an outlier and learn why clocking up 10,000 hours will help you succeed in Malcolm Gladwell's *Outliers: The Story of Success.*

Struggling in an extroverted world? Introverts are enjoying a renaissance, fuelled in part by Susan Cain's terrific bestseller, *Quiet: The Power of Introverts in a World That Can't Stop Talking.*

Copy-cat your way to success with Austin Kleon's great book, *Steal Like An Artist.*

Roll up your sleeves and bring out the big guns to win your creative battle with *The War of Art* by Steven Pressfield.

Power up with a new personality—read Breaking the Habit of Being Yourself: How to Lose Your Mind and Create a New One by Dr. Joe Dispenza.

Unleash the power of your mind by reading *You Are the Placebo: Making Your Mind Matter,* by Dr. Joe Dispenza.

Manifest your prosperity with Rhonda Byrne in her popular book, *The Secret.*

Ensure you don't starve by reading Jeff Goins collated wisdom in *Real Artists Don't Starve: Timeless Strategies for Thriving in the New Creative Age*.

Fortify your faith with Julia Cameron's book, *Faith and Will.*

How to Survive and Thrive in Any Life Crisis, Dr. Al Siebert

Thrive: The Third Metric to Redefining Success and Creating a Happier Life, Arianna Huffington

(This book has great content throughout and some excellent resources listed in the back.)

The Power of Now: A Guide to Spiritual Enlightenment, Eckhart Tolle

The Book of Joy, The Dalai Lama and Archbishop Desmond Tutu

The Sleep Revolution: Transforming Your Life One Night at a Time, Arianna Huffington

Quiet the Mind: An Illustrated Guide on How to Meditate, Mathew Johnstone

Comfortable with Uncertainty: 108 Teachings on Cultivating Fearlessness and Compassion, Pema Chodron

Power vs. Force: The Hidden Determinants of Human Behavior, David R. Hawkins

Learn how to live an inspired life with Tarot cards and other oracles. Read Jessa Crispin's book, *The Creative Tarot: A Modern Guide to an Inspired Life.*

Check out all of Collette-Baron-Reid's books, including: *Uncharted: The Journey Through Uncertainty to Infinite Possibility* and *Messages from Spirit: The Extraordinary Power of Oracles, Omens, and Signs.*

Embrace your fears—find nirvana by making peace with all that worries you in Marine Corps Veteran and author Akshay Nanavati's book, *Fearvana: The Revolutionary Science of How to Turn Fear into Health, Wealth and Happiness.*

STAY IN TOUCH

Become a fan and Continue To Be Supported, Encouraged, and Inspired

Subscribe to my newsletter and follow me on BookBub (https://www.bookbub.com/profile/cassandra-gaisford) and be the first to know about my new releases and giveaways

www.cassandragaisford.com
www.facebook.com/powerfulcreativity
www.instagram.com/cassandragaisford
www.youtube.com/cassandragaisfordnz
www.pinterest.com/cassandraNZ
www.linkedin.com/in/cassandragaisford
www.twitter.com/cassandraNZ

And please, do check out some of my videos where I share strategies and tips to stress less and love life more—http://www.youtube.com/cassandragaisfordnz

BLOG

Subscribe and be inspired by regular posts to help you increase your wellness, follow your bliss, slay self-doubt, and sustain healthy habits.

Learn more about how to achieve happiness and success at work and life by visiting my blog:

www.cassandragaisford.com/archives

SPEAKING EVENTS

Cassandra is available internationally for speaking events aimed at wellness strategies, motivation, inspiration and as a keynote speaker.

She has an enthusiastic, humorous and passionate style of delivery and is celebrated for her ability to motivate, inspire and enlighten.

For information navigate to www.cassandragaisford.com/contact/speaking

To ask Cassandra to come and speak at your workplace or conference, contact: cassandra@cassandragaisford.com

NEWSLETTERS

For inspiring tools and helpful tips subscribe to Cassandra's free newsletters here:

http://www.cassandragaisford.com

Sign up now and receive a free eBook to help you find your passion and purpose!

http://eepurl.com/bEArfT

ACKNOWLEDGMENTS

Thank you to Leonardo da Vinci for inspiring me, and to all the other authors and Leonardo experts I learned from as I wrote this book.

To all the wonderful people who took The Art of Success Questionnaire. Thank you for your honesty. Your responses were inspiring and your worries and concerns helped shape this book.

Thank you to all the advance readers. Your willingness to help, cheerleading and constructive feedback definitely made this book more successful.

Thank you too, for purchasing and reading this book. I hope you enjoyed it and that you'll be encouraged to follow your path with heart and dare to be different.

And to the love of my life—Lorenzo, my Templar Knight. Thank you for believing in me.

Thank you for trusting me to guide you. I really hope you

loved this book as much as I truly enjoyed writing it. And I hope it aids your success, as I have succeeded and flourished during the many hours I spent writing *The Art of Success.*

Here's to an extra-ordinary level of happiness and success in all lives.

Thank you so much!

Passionately yours in gratitude and love

COPYRIGHT

Copyright © 2020 Cassandra Gaisford
Published by Blue Giraffe Publishing 2020

Blue Giraffe Publishing is a division of Worklife Solutions Ltd.

Cover Design by Cassandra Gaisford

All rights reserved. No part of this publication may be repro-
duced, distributed, or transmitted in any form or by any
means, including photocopying, recording, or other electronic
or mechanical methods, without the prior written permission
of the author or publisher, except in the case of brief quota-
tions embodied in reviews and certain other non-commercial
uses permitted by copyright law.

Neither the publisher nor the author are engaged in rendering
professional advice or services to the individual reader. The
ideas, procedures, and suggestions contained in this book are

not intended as a substitute for psychotherapy, counselling, or consulting with your physician.

The intent of the author is only to offer information of a general nature to help you in your quest for emotional, physical, and spiritual well-being.

Any use of information in this book is at the reader's discretion and risk. Neither the author nor the publisher can be held responsible for any loss, claim or damage arising out of the use, or misuse, of the suggestions made, the failure to take medical advice or for any material on third party websites.

ISBN PRINT: 978-0-9941314-5-4

ISBN EBOOK: 978-0-9951072-1-2

ISBN HARDCOVER: 978-1-99-002017-9

First Edition